Showing Your True Colours

Fourteen stories of people who figured out why they were born and learned to live their truth - and how you can too

Michael E Daly

2022

Showing Your True Colours

Fourteen stories of people who figured out why they were born and learned to live their truth - and how you can too

First Edition: August 2022

ISBN 978-1-908293-62-6

Genius Media 2022

© Michael E Daly 2021

Author has asserted his rights under the Copyright, Designs and Patents act 1988 to be identified as the author of this work.

All rights reserved in all media. This book may not be copied, stored, transmitted or reproduced in any format or medium without specific prior permission from the author. Contact Genius Media for information about wholesale orders and review copies.

Cover artwork by Emma Freeth based on an original concept from Michael E Daly.

Genius Media

B1502

PO Box 15113

Birmingham

B2 2NJ

www.geniusmedia.pub

books@geniusmedia.pub

Contents

About the Author..4
   Praise for *Showing your True Colours*..............................4
   Praise for *Conversations in Singapore*............................6
   Praise for *The Six Traits of Self-leadership*.....................6

Dedication..8

Foreword..9

Showing Your True Colours...11

1. Become the Captain of Your Own Ship.............................16

2. Being a Leading Light..21
   The inner journey...22
   How, then, do you figure out why you were born?...........27
   The outer journey...33

3. Rise and Shine...39
   Figuring out why they were born....................................46

4. Don't Rock the Boat...55

5. Cracking On..75

6. The Right Tack..95

7. Forging Ahead..103

Epilogue..116

Acknowledgements...117

About the Author

Michael E. Daly spent nearly a decade living, studying, and training to be a monk in Ireland. Today, as well as being an acclaimed author, he is a broadcaster and talk show host, an NLP Master Practitioner and holds qualifications in Social Care, Entrepreneurship and Enterprise, Innovation, Public Administration and Health Care Management. He is the author of the critically acclaimed The Six Traits of Self-Leadership: How to Create a Life of Success and Happiness and Conversations in Singapore: Searching for True Success on the Silk Road One Question at a Time.

Praise for *Showing your True Colours*

'I wholeheartedly recommend this engaging and enjoyable book to anyone that might be questioning what to do with their life – stop what you are doing and read it! It is full of the wisdom of ordinary people who have woken up to their potential, braced themselves for the punches and come out on top!'

Brian Colbert, author of The Happiness Habit and co-founder of The Irish institute of NLP.

'Open Michael's book and learn that there is another way – and that it is up to us all to make change happen if we want a better world.'

Professor Peter Herrmann, Research Fellow at the Human Rights Centre, Central South University, Changsha, China.

'The COVID-19 crisis has caused many people to reconsider the meaning of their life and how they want to live it. Fundamental changes to our working life have enabled people to relocate their homes, to change jobs or to dramatically alter their choice of career. For anyone seeking to find the courage to make similar choices, reading Showing Your True Colours will give you the strength to live your future life on your terms.'

Professor Thomas M. Cooney, Technological University Dublin (TU Dublin), Ireland.

'If you want to live a life filled with meaning, read this inspirational book full of motivating stories from real people. Michael has such amazing experience in helping people to discover their true self on this journey called "life".'

Associate Professor Marina Ochkovskaya, Lomonosov Moscow State University, Russia.

'Aristotle said, "Know thyself and become what you are", and Michael follows that great thought. His book is full of inspiring stories of the journeys that people made to find themselves and the destinations they wanted to bring their life and work to. They show that God's plan is there, waiting to be found and then pursued so that you can thrive and flourish, and when you do so will all those around you. A great read!'

Professor Przemek Zbierowski, University of Economics, Katowice, Poland.

Praise for *Conversations in Singapore*

'A modern fable, which echoes the story-telling style of Paolo Coelho.'

Sophie Grenham, Irish Times

'Unique and easy to learn from as Michael brings together all his experiences from his travels and teachings, as well as his life as a monk.'

Chinedu Onyejelem, Metro Eireann

'A short book, but one which you will return to many times […] for the important questions it raises.'

Eoin Meegan, NewsFour

'In this new classic, Michael Daly invites the reader to consider how to live a life worth living […] this book will leave the reader to discover a thousand and one tales of who they can be.'

Professor Jerry Gale, Director of the Family Therapy Doctoral Program, University of Georgia, USA

Praise for *The Six Traits of Self-Leadership*

'One of the smartest books you will ever get to read.'

Professor Jim Blythe, Cardiff, Wales

'Have you ever asked the question: "What do I need to be successful?" […] In order to understand more, read this book!'

Professor Gerd Mühlenbeck, Heidelberg, Germany

'I recently experienced two moments of enlightenment – listening to Michael's lectures and reading his book on self-leadership […] You cannot remain at the same stage of your life journey as you were before opening the first pages of this book.'

Jolanta Preidiene, Head of IRO, Vilnius University of Applied Sciences, Lithuania

'An outstanding prescription for getting the kind of satisfaction we want from our lives.'

Professor Alan Zimmerman, City University of New York, USA

To learn more about Michael's books, you can email Michael personally or visit his website.

michael@michaeldalyireland.com

www.michaeldalyireland.com

Dedication

For all those who have figured out why they were born and gone to live it.

For their passion and willingness to engage their minds, follow their hearts and make this world a better place – as they make a difference to us all through their unique contributions.

Foreword

There's a story of a chicken farmer who found an eagle's egg. He put it under a hen and soon the egg hatched.

The young eagle grew up with all the other chickens and whatever they did, the eagle did too. He thought he was a chicken, just like them. Since the chickens could only fly for a short distance, the eagle also learnt to fly a short distance. He thought that was what he was supposed to do. So that was all that he thought he could do. As a result, that was all he was able to do.

One day, the eagle saw a bird flying high above him. He was very impressed. "Who is that?" he asked the hens.

"That's the eagle, the king of the birds," the hens told him. "He belongs to the sky. We belong to the earth; we're just chickens." So, the eagle believed the other chickens. He lived and died as a chicken, that's what he thought he was.

Carl Jung would call the bird's fate "the hypnosis of social conditioning".

It is said that it's choice, not chance, that brings about a genuine change in people. Michael Daly has written a beautiful book, Showing Your True Colours, about people who have all had the courage to make those life-changing choices to live lives true to themselves. A book about those who dared to fly out of the chicken coops of their comfortable lives.

The greatest enemy of our human potential is the comfort zone, for all the magic of life happens outside it. This has been the brilliant discovery for those people whose stories are shared in Showing Your True Colours.

Leo Tolstoy's story 'The Death of Ivan Ilyich' describes the life of Ivan, a High Court judge in nineteenth-century Russia. He despises his work and at the end of his life, he is faced with a question: "What if my entire life has been wrong?" Similarly, when Bonnie Ware was researching her book The Top Five Regrets of the Dying, she found the No 1 regret was: "I wish I'd had the courage to live a life true to myself, not the life others expected of me."

I remember the great Dr Pearse Lyons, president and CEO of Alltech, telling an audience of over 3,000 people in Kentucky to "connect to your purpose, to connect to that music inside of you, not to die with your music still inside you …" Then he paused, looked across all those faces from countries all over the globe, and finished, "Do what makes your heart sing."

The people telling their stories in Showing Your True Colours have all had the courage to break out for their comfort zones and do what makes their hearts sing. They are modern-day eagles soaring across the sky. On their deathbeds, they will sing with Edith Piaf, "Non, je ne regrette rien." No, I regret nothing. I did what made my heart sing.

Now go and read this book and let your heart sing.

Declan Coyle, author of The Green Platform

Showing Your True Colours

In the summer of 1999, I was fortunate enough to go on a sailing holiday with someone I had met the previous summer. My new friend wanted to learn to sail, whereas I had no great desire to do so. Only, as the holiday went on, the sailing became more and more enjoyable. Towards the end of the week, I realised that this was something I wanted to pursue – that this was the perfect holiday and sailing was the perfect hobby for me. The sailing holiday was in so many ways life-changing in that it gave me a completely new social outlet, a hobby I loved, a new skill to learn and a superb way to switch off and enjoy nature at its best. It is for this reason that I have used sailing terms for both the title of this book and as the heading for each chapter. 'Showing your true colours', for example, is a sailing term that has come to mean revealing one's true intentions. The 'colours' of a ship are its flags and to 'show your true colours' refers to lowering any flags that are intended to deceive others and raising the flags of the sovereign that the ship really serves. In this book, it refers to showing the world who you were born to be.

The sailing holiday also brought home to me how we often have our best insights or stumble across a profound truth about ourselves in the quietest of moments, regardless of what it is we are doing. Maybe for you it is when you get some hard-earned space to go for a walk or are simply able to take some time out to relax from your heavy workload or busy schedule. It could be while you're doing the garden or cooking, if that's something you enjoy, or maybe even when you just get a few moments of peace to have a shower or have time for a bath. With this in mind, will you please allow yourself a few quiet moments now to read and reflect on the stories that I am going to be sharing in this book?

These are the stories of people who figured out why they were born and the work they were put here to do; they are about people who are now living extraordinary lives in the most ordinary of ways. This book and their stories are about showing you how you can be just like them. You too can live your best life, having figured out why you were born and the work you are meant to be doing, which will soon have you showing your true colours as you become the captain of your own ship.

At some point, most of us want to know what life is all about and why are we here. Or more importantly, why we were born and what are we here to do. Mark Twain is often misquoted as saying: 'The two most important days in your life are the day you are born and the day you find out why.' Whereas he would surely have said: 'The three most important days in your life are the day you were born, the day you find out why and the day you then go live it!'

People have asked me countless times, 'For what reason was I born and what do I need to be working at?' Every time, my answer is the same: 'I don't know, for how could I? If you do not know why you were born and the work you need to be doing, what would make you think that I know?' This is the case for you too: I cannot give you a reason as to why you were born and what work you need to be doing, but I can help you find your own answers.

So how do you figure out why you were born and what work you need to be doing? This is a very different question, which this book will help you to address. In fact, it will go much further, as it will also invite you to consider what might be stopping you from living the life you were born to live and doing the work you should be doing. And it will suggest how you can successfully overcome these obstacles.

How can I promise you all of this? Well, for the simple reason that I lived, trained and studied to be a monk for nearly a decade, along with my knowledge gained from over thirty-plus years of working with people to enable them to answer these sorts of questions, and what I discovered about the meaning of true success by driving halfway around the world, from London to Sydney along the Silk Road. All of these experiences have enabled me to write this book and share the stories of other people just like you, who have found their own answers – as you will too, having finished it. Yes, that really can be the case. Having discovered why you were born and what you were put here to do, you give yourself the best chance of living the life you want.

The stories and the tellers of them will most likely challenge you, yet they will also get you imagining. They will give you hope, inspiration, and above all else, encourage you to figure out why you were born and the work you need to be doing to live your best life. The stories also show that having decided to follow their true calling, these people often had no idea how everything was going to work out for them. It was a challenge to leave behind their old lives, for it often meant losing the security and safety that went with doing what they knew. While knowing what they wanted to do with their life and work, many of them were not sure how achievable this would be. At some point, they had to take a leap of faith from the life they were living to the life they wanted to live. And living their new life affected all areas of their existence – their health, relationships, wealth, work, hobbies, interests and the legacy they will now leave behind. This can be the case for you too.

If, like them, you want to take that leap from your old life towards the life you want to be living then, just as they did, you will have to muster up courage. As there is no easy way to take that leap, it will require you to have hope, imagination and trust in yourself and in your God if you have one. Just like those telling their stories here, you too were put on this earth to fulfil a unique purpose and leave a legacy. Yes, it can be a challenge to ask yourself why you were born. Yet if you are prepared to put the time, effort and energy into figuring this out, it can often be simply answered. It is in the living out of your answer where the real work will start. For when you figure out why you were born and then go live it, you really are giving yourself the greatest chance to enjoy your best life possible.

Well then, are you ready to live a new life? A different life? A better life? If so, let the storytellers in these pages show you how they came to figure out:

- Why they were born and the work they were meant to be doing;
- What challenges could have stopped them from going and living their new life;
- How they were able to overcome these challenges;
- The ways in which they are now living the life they were born to live and doing the work they want.

If, just like them, you want to do all of this yourself, let's throw off the bowlines and get started…

1. Become the Captain of Your Own Ship

Make the Choice to Change

Maybe you are thinking you are too young to change and that you will get to experience the life you were born to live at a later stage? If so, let's start with the story of Danny Range (the name by which he is now better known) from Ohio, who at the age of twenty-four decided he was done with being a burnout. He was sick of being high all the time. Sick of being out of shape. Sick of throwing his life away to the carefree party lifestyle. Nearly fifty pounds overweight, with crippling credit card debt and less than $300 to his name, on 12 January 2016 he looked into the mirror with fury in his eyes and declared there and then that he was officially committed to turning his life around. A promise that he followed up the very next day by making the same commitment publicly via social media and letting everybody how he was now going to dedicate his life to being an author, speaker, and film writer. He tells me:

> I had always dreamt of writing a book and having it turned into a movie. So I portrayed it to people, like, 'I'm going to go do this', and made it sound like a business

thing that I was going to do. Only what I was really doing at the time was clamouring for and trying to hold on to hope, for I really had nothing – including having no money, losing my friends – and I had nothing else in life, other than a dream to write, which gave me something to hold on to.

Knowing that I had to sit in this space and learn how to write – because I didn't know what else to do, and just did not want to get back into drugs – I locked myself into that basement and wrote and kept writing. Looking back on it now, it was the greatest move I ever made in my life, as I told everybody I'm going to dedicate my life to being an author and speaker. And having done so, I then had to go and do it.

He goes on to tell me:

I locked myself in the basement, where I was pretty much alone that year, and I wrote a 250,000-word book – and it proved to be the best thing I ever did. Even if it sucked!

I was just so naïve, driven and arrogant, having finished writing the book, and nothing was going to hold me back. Now, not knowing how things in the publishing world worked, I rang agents and publishers. To always be told the same thing: send us an email setting out what your book is about, etc. I kept ringing, finally getting through and talking to Joel Goetler, the person who discovered Jordan Belfort, the 'Wolf of Wall Street'.

We talk and he can tell I'm driven and heading places. I also get the sense he is also kind of laughing in the back of his mind, knowing that I have so much to learn. Only he says, 'All right, send me the book.' I do and having sent it I am even more arrogant, for I believe he will be right back, offering me a deal. He does come right back to me, saying it sucks and to use it as a learning experience and to go write another book.

Taking on board his advice and having been humbled by the entire experience, Danny went and wrote another book, Make Success Your Addiction. He says:

> The next book was an apology pretty much to everyone who read the first one expecting more of my advice, as pretty much everyone's reaction to the first book was: 'Yeah, you've lived a crazy life. We get that and we really liked the last chapter, which gave great motivational advice. And we want more of that.' And I was like, well, I want to write a book which can be turned into a movie, so in fact they didn't want the second book that I wanted to write as I wanted it to be a work of fiction.
>
> But I gave them the book they wanted – I went and wrote it. Thirty percent of them bought it and it was a complete failure. Lesson learnt: do not live your life and your brand based on what people want.

Taking the lessons learnt, he now accepts that he is a fiction writer, and that this is the type of writing for him. He tells me:

I was born and raised in Warren, Ohio, to parents who were in their late teens, and I moved from home to home with my mother throughout my childhood. Living in a cockroach-covered apartment at one time. So, yes, I am driven and not afraid of hard work, which I knew it would take to write a new book that could be turned into a film.

Therefore, in the middle of a public statement via social media, I declared that I would now land a movie deal for a novel that I was now going to write. I chose to make my own success my choice of addiction – and this can be the case for others if they so choose. And, yes, I choose to fight and never ever give up. [My life] is dedicated to showing the world that you can make your wildest dreams come true if you are prepared to put in the work. That you can have happiness, great health, and be the richest version of yourself.

For I believe I am living proof that persistence and hard work, along with having a healthy routine, can have you turn your life around at any age into a success story. For as you know, Michael, my novel, 422: Scandalous – a book that shares a grisly message about what can happen if you don't take your mental health seriously – has officially been optioned to be made into a film.

As we finish talking, Danny tells me:

I'm not special, nor are any of my accomplishments. While my comeback was a personal goal at first, it has developed into something much more meaningful: a powerful message of hope for people who want to change their lives around and pursue the life they truly want to be living. The dream for me now is to be involved in all aspects of the business of making a film: from having written the script to rising finance, casting, producing and even acting in it. To then in turn use the profits from this new career to open up a chain of businesses that will create jobs for countless people around the United States.

As a man who, in his early life, was called an 'addict' and a 'low-life' amongst so many other derogatory terms, Danny Range is proud to be known now as a workhorse and a leader. In addition, as you listen to 'Warren's Finest' you just know the world is his oyster and you truly want to wish him the very best, for he really is one of the good guys. He was not going to let his age, inexperience or upbringing hold him back from doing what he truly wanted to be doing with his life and work – so could that be the case for you too, whether you are young or old? Can you be the leading light in your own life?

2. Being a Leading Light

Discover why you were born

Many of us like to believe in the existence of eureka moments in which we'll suddenly come to understand why we were born and what we need to be doing with our life to make it a success. The storytellers in these pages will tell you it rarely ever goes down that way. They will tell you that while there may have been no one overriding eureka moment, there was a whole sequence of insights instead. Moreover, it was these insights that inspired them to figure out why they were born and the life they now wanted to live if it were to be one of real success for them. For many of them, it was a case of:

> First insight: they were at a place in their life but it was not where they wanted to be.
>
> Second insight: they had to admit this to themselves if they were to have any chance of their life getting better.
>
> Third insight: they knew they would have to take ownership of the life they were living and figure out why they were born if they wanted things to change.
>
> Fourth insight: they needed now to accept that they would have to go and live the life they were born to live if they were to be true to themselves and have a life worth living.

The storytellers accepted that they had gotten themselves into a situation of living a life that had mostly lost its sense of meaning and purpose for them – the two key ingredients to a joyful and productive life. They also now knew that if they wanted a different and better life than the one they were currently living, then they had to do something about it if they wanted anything to change. That it was their responsibility to go and make the change happen, even if they had no idea how they were going to do this.

The Inner Journey

The first step to changing the storytellers' lives involved acknowledging that they were not where they wanted to be in life. They then accepted that it was up to them and them alone to do something about it. But what is it that makes people begin to question the life they are living? Often, it might be a milestone event, such as being made redundant. Or it could involve doing a course or committing to work on personal growth and development. It could even mean deciding to actively pursue a dream. Yet for many people, it can involve a period of ill health, as was the case for Steven Farrell.

Steven had pretty much done everything right in his life. He did not do drugs or smoke, and only had an occasional drink. As well as spending time in the gym, he did a physical workout every morning. Even his hobbies included the healthy pursuit of horse riding. He maintained a balanced diet and was a vegetarian. Living such a healthy lifestyle, not for one moment did he believe that cancer would ever affect him. Yet 11 September 2017 was to become a date he would never forget, for on that day his life was to change forever when he was diagnosed with stage 3 metastatic melanoma, the deadliest form of skin cancer, caused by UV rays from the sun.

When the doctor told him the awful news, it hit him like a ton of bricks and he passed out. His husband, Eamon, and the doctor took care of him, which meant that he could then hear the good news. If his cancer had been diagnosed any later, he would probably have died. But having it diagnosed at this stage, along with having surgery, would mean a 95 percent survival rate. He was one of the lucky ones. His was a type of cancer that people in relationships often spot early on because their partner notices it, just as his husband had in Steven's case. At the same time, Steven knew how serious it was, as this had him ending up lying in the intensive care unit. With this came the realisation that he had not yet reached his full potential. There was so much more he could do with his life and work. As he told me:

> It was only when I was lying on my bed in intensive care that I realised there is only one of me. That we only get one shot at this life of ours. That I needed to be nicer and kinder to myself. That it was now time for all the negative self-talk and limiting beliefs to go.
>
> There was also a real inner change with the realisation that I needed to push myself, because I hadn't been. There was so much more that I could do in my life and work. For if I died at that point, it would have been the most painful death imaginable: it would have been a regretful death. A painful and emotionally charged death.

> For there I was, lying in the hospital bed, knowing that I had never realised my potential and that this was down to laziness and procrastination.
>
> I genuinely accepted that if I got to live to be eighty or ninety or beyond, then when I am on my deathbed it just cannot be then as it was now, as I lay there at thirty-four years of age. Moreover, with that came the realisation that I am getting a second chance to live my life. That if I take it, then when I die at least I will be able to say to myself, 'Yes, I gave it my best. I tried it all and have exhausted myself in doing so.'

This realisation, along with being the spiritual person that he is, made him accept that it was time to grab hold of his life and move on. So, with a thought and a prayer to a higher power, he decided it was now time to live by his new motto:

'If You Want to Do Something, Then Do It Now!'

Once Steven left hospital, there was no more time for worrying about what others were thinking or thought of him; being an artist, he was no longer just going to paint what others wanted. While it had never been part of his plan before, he decided that he would give talks and deliver workshops about goals and goal-setting in pursuit of achieving your dreams – just as he continues to do in his own life and work. He pursued further personal development and training, and qualified as an NLP (neuro-linguistic programming) mind coach – a skill which he uses in his work with clients today, enabling them to overcome challenges, set and achieve their goals and live life on their own terms.

Steven now also podcasts, which he loves. This, along with his talks, has him sharing his message on the world stage, and his work sees him spending more time travelling both in Ireland and overseas. All of which means that his work and his world truly have expanded. With that being so, he decided to take a step back from politics, which he had previously been involved in, as it was not possible to be as active politically as he would have liked. Yet he will always make time to advocate for the rights of minority groups and, being the person that he is, you just know that this will always be the case.

Regarding his original cancer diagnosis, he now has the 'all clear'. Other than the pain, worry and heartache that his family and friends went through, he says he would not change a thing. All that happened has made him the person he is, and as he says himself: 'I wouldn't be who I am and getting to live a life that I love, if it hadn't been for all that I have gone through – including the cancer.'

He believes that we are all here for a purpose and that he is now living his. For he is getting to do what he truly wants to do with his life and work, as through sharing his story he now enables others to discover and then go live their own purpose. In addition to being a story about dealing with and overcoming cancer, his experience shows the importance of creative expression and how it can help people deal with any difficulty or challenge. Steven's creativity has helped him through the toughest periods of his life, including grown up gay in a working-class part of Dublin. He tells me, 'I am getting to live the dream as I now work with people in a way that has me using my creativity, be it through my podcasts, goal-setting workshops or the book I am writing – all types of work that enable others to live their purpose and pursue the dreams they have for their own life and work.'

As to the future, yes, he will continue to go on living his purpose and doing the work he truly wants to be doing. He will keep sharing his story and motivating people to act now to work towards their goals and dreams. In addition, he will go on encouraging people to make memories with the people they love, before it is too late.

His insights apply to you too: are you going to go on living the life you are living, or live the life you were born to live? If you can answer 'yes' to any or all of the following questions, then you have a decision to make:

- ✔ Do you have a sense there could be more to life than the one you are living?

- ✔ Do you believe you could be living a different and better life than the one you have?

- ✔ Are you now in a place in your life where you just don't want to be?

- ✔ Do you believe that you are not being true to yourself through the life you are living and the work you are doing?

- ✔ Would you like the life you are living to be happier?

- ✔ Are you ready for more satisfaction in your life?

- ✔ Do you really want to be living the life you were born to live and doing the work you would love to do?

If you have answered 'yes' to any or indeed all of these questions, it is now time for you to take ownership of your life. For when you do, it will be possible to figure out why you were born. Again, this is all about going on an inner journey; an inner journey of transformation with initially no extraordinary outward changes, as you come to know why you were born and what it is you are meant to be doing with your life.

HOW, THEN, DO YOU FIGURE OUT WHY YOU WERE BORN?

You can figure out why you were born by:

1. Coming to know what you are strong at, and then
2. Where you can put your strengths to best use in your life and work.

For when you do this, you will be giving yourself the best chance to live your life as a leading light both for yourself and for all those around you. (The phrase 'leading light' comes from a sailing term for a pair of beacons used in navigation; it now means someone who shows the way or is a leader in their own right.)

What, then, are you strong at? Now, what I mean here by 'strength' and 'being strong' relates to those activities that make you feel strong and capable when you are carrying them out. These feelings may be found in activities in which you exhibit consistent, near perfect performance. They are those activities that you do well and for which you retain a powerful appetite. They feel easy, like you need not try very hard. Perhaps they proved simple for you to pick up and you learnt them quickly. Your strengths feel innate and come from within; they are something that you find easy to tie in to, to use, to grow and develop. When you are using your strengths, you do not struggle to concentrate. Instead, you naturally stay focused and time speeds up, and as you carry on using them you continue to feel focused and time speeds up even more.

So, if you want to figure out why you were born and what you are meant to be doing with your life, start noticing the activities that when you are doing them, they…

- Seem to come so naturally to you, it is almost as if you are not even trying when you do them;
- Make you feel 'in the flow' and you can focus easily on whatever it is you are doing;
- Keep your interest and your concentration with almost no effort;
- Leave you feeling strong, fulfilled and powerful;
- Draw you back to them repeatedly;
- Hold your attention and you enjoy doing them;
- Inspire you to keep volunteering to do them.

Knowing where your strengths lie by identifying the activities that come naturally to you, and where best you can use them, means you have figured out why you were born. The next step is to create the life that allows you to use these activities.

The choice, then, is to stay where you are in your life or to set off on an outer journey – a journey whereby you use your strengths to make the life you want to be living become an everyday reality for yourself. As was the case for Daniela Enzinger.

Growing up in Austria and with languages not really being her forte at school, Daniela did not get to become the schoolteacher she had originally wanted to be. Instead, she finished school at seventeen and, inspired by a desire to help people, along with a curiosity for travel, she trained to be a hotel assistant. As the Austrian hospitality sector had such an excellent reputation, she knew that if she ever wanted to leave Austria, this would be a great way out. She tells me:

> When I finished my apprenticeship, I received some money from my grandparents. This allowed me to celebrate turning twenty-one by travelling to Nepal and the USA on holidays in 2001. It was a brilliant experience as I really enjoyed learning about other cultures. I also got to realise that there was so much more out there than just the world in which I had grown up.

On returning to Austria and her job as a receptionist at a hotel in Salzburg, Daniela knew it was time to search for work abroad. This led to her being offered a job with a beautiful 4-star manor house hotel in Surrey, just outside London, in August 2003.

In 2011, she returned to Nepal on holiday. While she was there, someone suggested that she should get a job in the hospitality sector in the Gulf as they paid Westerners really well. She looked into it and a few months later she received a job offer from a family-run hotel in Qatar, where she moved in April 2012. She says of the experience:

It was a tough time there, Michael. For I'd been told that the job I was getting was in one of the best hotels, with one of the best restaurants. Neither was true, and I was also promised so many other things, but in reality, the hotel had so many cockroaches that when you opened the door, all you saw was them running away. Likewise, the promise about accommodation and excellent working conditions never happened. Only I stuck with it. Eventually, a new owner took over and things improved. I worked hard and ended up becoming joint general manager, before moving back to the UK in September 2014. There, I worked part-time in the hotel I had been employed in before travelling to Qatar, so that I could finish my master's degree.

She explains:

Just before travelling to Qatar, I had started to study for a Master's in International Security, like I said, as I felt ready for a new challenge and wanted to see if I could use all that I had learnt to date to help others in a different way. So, with my love for travel and meeting people from different cultures and backgrounds, it seemed as if there were a lot of opportunities within that area of work. Only, around that time, I also got to see a programme on TV about the Israel–Palestine conflict through the eyes of a British soldier who had served in Palestine at the end of World War Two. This was to change both my life and my course of study – which I switched to a Master's in Human Rights and Global Ethics. For I'd come to realise that many human rights violations were taking place in the name of international security.

I started to see so many injustices that were going on in the world. A seed was planted, as I wanted to be part of the solution and not a part of this problem.

I knew it would be very challenging to move away from the tourism and hospitality sector in which I had made my career and to get a job with a non-for-profit organisation dealing with injustices.

When Daniela finished her master's degree in 2014, she was at a certain income level professionally and also had a student loan to repay. This meant she could not really afford to take a pay cut and get an entry-level job within the not-for-profit sector.

Yet she was determined not to let this hold her back, for she knew it was up to her to find a way forwards if she wanted to become a leading light in her own life and work in her chosen area. So, playing to the strengths that she had developed and honed while working in the tourism and hospitality sector, she got a job in 2015 at a human rights law firm as their office manager. She believed that having the words 'human rights' on her CV would assist her in getting a job within the not-for-profit sector. As proved to be the case, for in 2017 she started working as the office manager for Lumos, the international charity founded by the author of Harry Potter, J. K. Rowling, which promotes an end to the institutionalisation of children worldwide. She tells me:

> It was great, Michael, for not long after starting, I expanded my role by taking on and doing some support work for our international offices. As Lumos expanded, a new operations manager's position was created. I applied and got the job. I loved it as it meant working closer with the programme's team and getting to travel to Latin America and the Caribbean. It was a brilliant time as I could set strategy, deliver training and get to share my knowledge and learn so much from the locals who were involved in rolling out our projects.

Then, when Daniela felt ready, she drew on all her experience and knowledge to land her dream job in January 2021 as Head of Operations with Reprieve, a not-for-profit international organisation that defends marginalised people who are facing human rights abuses, often at the hands of powerful governments.

As you listen to Daniela talk (and despite the fact that she once thought she wasn't good at languages, that is not the case now – for her English is excellent), you just know this is where she will become a leading light. Yet she has never given up on her dream of one day becoming a teacher, for as I ask her about the future, she tells me:

> Michael, I stuck with it and never gave up. I got to study and do a master's degree in a topic that just came so easily to me. This led to me wanting to work in the not-for-profit sector. So, having loved what I studied and because I am enjoying my work so much, I have not ruled out doing a PhD. Which might just have me one day teaching at a university.

As Daniela continues to play to her strengths and to do the right thing by herself, those around her and the world, you get the sense that one day she will get to achieve that childhood dream of becoming a teacher.

THE OUTER JOURNEY

When you decide to live your life using your strengths, it is then all about the outer work of living the life you were born to live. This was the case for Tom Dalton who, having finished school in 2004, decided to go to college and study Sound Recording and Music Technology. The course seemed an excellent fit for him as he is dyslexic, something which he has embraced, learnt from and made the most of.

After Tom finished college at the age of twenty in 2006, an opportunity arose for him to travel to Canada. He was delighted to go. It was a chance to gain new experiences, as well as visit an unknown country. He would not let this brilliant opportunity pass by and he grasped it. Being the outgoing people's person that he is, it proved to be a magnificent experience as he got to work in a variety of jobs and have a marvellous time there.

In 2007, when his visa was up, he returned to what was to be the start of an economic recession in Ireland. Drawing on the experience he had gained from his time in Vancouver, he got a job in retail. Within a brief period, he moved into a supervisory role and then into a management position. All the while, he continued to read self-growth and personal development books, which he had been doing since a young age. Then, in 2014, while still working part-time, he went back to college to study his genuine passion: exercise, nutrition and sport.

By the time he finished his course the following year, the opportunity was still there for him to go back to work full-time and make a lifelong career within the retail industry. The only thing was that while in college he got to teach classes on physical fitness and wellbeing – and loved it. This had him starting to ask himself whether he could make a career out of teaching these sorts of classes. He sought advice on this and the feedback was that he should stick with the retail industry, for it was hard to make a living, let alone build a career within the sports and fitness industry. But as Tom told me:

> The only thing was, even with all feedback telling me how difficult it would be to make a living within this industry, I just knew that this was where I wanted to make my mark. If that were to happen, then it would mean having to give up my job in retail and the potential career that would have been available to me, and to start to work for myself. To set up my own business – as this was the only viable option of making a decent living. Only this was scary, very scary because it meant having to turn my back on a guaranteed income.

This made him ask himself, 'Why would I want to walk away from all this?' – a question he was to ask of himself many times. The thing was that he really enjoyed the positive feedback he was receiving from the classes he was giving and this had him answering:

That, yes, I can stay in the corner safe and not get to do anything that I really want to do in life. This may well be the case for so many others, only I really did not want this to be the case for me.

So, yes, afraid and all that I was. I had to walk away from the job I was doing and give it my best to make a successful business out of doing the work I love. Now, knowing that I could always go back and get a job in retail if it did not work out, gave me some sense of relief. Yet this did not give me any comfort from my biggest fear at that time. A fear I can now laugh at. For it still happens – simply because I put myself and the business out there so much; it was the fear of rejection and 'what then?' I knew that this work could have such a brilliant and positive impact on so many people. Only what if people did not agree and rejected it?

Dealing with and overcoming the fear and the 'what then?' was something I knew had to be faced if I was to live the reason I was born and do the work I wanted to be doing. So, I did – only now when the rejection does happen, it drives me on more. The 'what then?' is now a case of 'right, let's get the feedback as to why a potential customer and business said no, learn from it and keep moving on to bigger, better and brighter things.'

With his parents' support as he was living at home (and this is something for which he is very grateful), he knew it was as good a time as ever to go for it financially. Sure, if it did not work out, as he said, he could always go back to retail!

He decided not to seek the advice or approval of anyone else. As he had big dreams and ambitions, he would now work on them, but he was afraid of putting them out there and having to deal with other people's reactions. Then, not letting the fear get in the way, he went for it, knowing that he would give it his all to ensure it become the success he believed it could be. He handed in his notice in late 2014 and his new company, TD Performance, became a reality, with the aim of motivating and educating individuals and workforces on all areas of fitness, nutrition and wellbeing.

The initial feedback was very positive and there seemed to be a real demand for what it was he was offering. He was on his way, working hard and, in his own words: 'With a bit of luck, the word got out there of the work I was doing. Through this word of mouth, the business went from strength to strength. This in turn had me asking: "How could I make this a business that will work for me, as opposed to me just working in the business?"' He met with his accountant and they put a structure in place for company growth: in 2020, TD Performance became a limited company and Tom was no longer working as a sole trader. Now, as he will tell you honestly, it took him over five years to get it to that point. He never thought for one moment when he left his job in 2014 that it would take as much work or so long to get to that point as it did.

His story, just like so many of the others telling their stories here, has not been a straight line in bringing him to where he is now. There have been difficulties, very many of them. Many rejections, a lot of frustration, bad days, good and brilliant days – along with loneliness, real loneliness. It may well be easier to have a 9 to 5 job,

Monday to Friday, with a guaranteed income, yet Tom loves the challenge of running his own company. So, having a 9 to 5 job is just not an option for him.

Yes, at times business can be slow. Only he really has learnt to treat it like a marathon and not a sprint. While this has been tough for him, it is a brilliant lesson to have learnt. He is also grateful for the opportunity to be his own boss, as this is something he loves. Likewise, he is very grateful for the opportunity to do work he loves – work that can make such a positive difference to so many peoples' lives.

On meeting Tom, you just know that he has so much to give. Doing what he is now doing has him giving of his best, playing to his strengths and getting to show his true colours.

You also know that this is something he will not give up lightly. Likewise, Tom's story also resonates with so many of the others telling their stories here, in that they are all trying to give themselves the greatest chance of success by following these principles and practices:

- Surrounding themselves with the right people;
- Reading the right books;
- Having a mentor if needs be;
- Being involved in a network or group that is best suited to supporting them in the life they wish to be leading;
- Putting strategies in place to deal with the loneliness (particularly so when starting out) in the best way possible;

- Facing their fears and accepting that, yes, they are taking a risk in going to do what they are doing, yet they believe it is a risk worth taking;
- Going for it once they have decided to go for it, and not just sitting around;
- Accepting that it is a marathon and not a sprint when pursuing the life they truly want to be living;
- Telling very few people of their intention to give up the life they have been living so as to be freer to live it (they might tell their partner if they are fortunate enough to have one who will support them);
- Asking for the support of others if this was something they needed, particularly when starting a new business.

Tom and the other storytellers leave you with a sense that their lives are going to go from strength and to strength. As they play to their strengths and get to rise and shine, this leads to them having such a positive impact on so many other people's lives, both now and in the future.

3. Rise and Shine

Let This Be Your Time

Are you ready to rise and shine – a sailing term meaning to wake up and be alert – by consciously choosing to seek out the life you were born to live? Many of our storytellers found themselves at a point where they knew they wanted to live a different life, a better life. For Kevin Gibson, it was because he had been born in the USA. He grew up in Ireland but always intended to travel back to the land of his birth one day. He finished school in 1989 and worked in custom clearance in Dublin, before going back to the USA in 1993, where he was employed mainly within the finance industry. While taking a holiday in Chicago in 1995, he was to meet, fall in love with and later marry Jeanne. It was there that they were to stay and raise a family, until Jeanne's tragic and untimely death in 2005 at the age of just thirty-five, two years after suffering a brain aneurysm. Not long after her death, Kevin and their three children moved back to Dublin to be closer to the rest of his family. On his return, he worked in sales within the software industry.

Jeanne's best friend Krissy, also born in Chicago, had gone to Los Angeles at the age of twenty-six to pursue a career in acting, having completed a degree in theatre studies. While there, she was to give it her best shot for ten years, only it was not to be. Her acting career did not go to plan nor work out how she would have liked. Realising where she could best make a contribution and impact in life, she moved to Ireland in 2006 – a country she had never been to before. Yet she had spent every day since Kevin's return reading stories to his and Jeanne's children over the internet, and she now wanted to do it in person and support them in whatever way she could. She aimed to make her living doing voice-overs from her new home in Dublin. Little did she know that she and Kevin would fall in love themselves, marry and have a baby in 2010.

As time went by, they came to realise that they needed to set up their own business if they were to have more time with their family and get greater satisfaction from their working lives. Equally, they told me of their belief that: 'As long as you're working for the man, there will always be a ceiling to what you can do and earn.' And they now wanted to be in a place where they could do their own thing and set their own ceiling.

Accepting this, it was agreed they would start their own business. But they faced many questions. What could they do? What would they enjoy doing? And what could they truly make a living from? After several years of brainstorming and talking about starting a business together, their ideas kept falling flat and coming to nothing. Yet they never gave up and just kept at it. They came to realise that the answer had been staring them in the face all the time.

For they kept coming back to their first idea, and that was always baking! This was for the simple reason that it was where Krissy's passion lay. She had loved baking ever since childhood, and it had always been her dream to open a bakery one day. She and Kevin now knew that if they were to choose anything to make a living from, then it surely had to be from baking, if for no other reason than it just felt so much a part of who Krissy was. Likewise, it involved a product they could produce and sell themselves.

The only problem was that along with the real financial fear of giving up their jobs and setting up a baking business, there lay another very real fear for Krissy. For she had a personal connection to the cakes and desserts that they would now be making if they set up the business. While, yes, she hoped that everyone would love them as much as she did, what if people did not? She had a recurring worry that mostly all the people who'd told her they loved her cakes and desserts, and that she should sell them, were friends and family. What if they were biased and just being nice to her? Also, it felt like she would be putting her heart on the line, because what if it did not work out and her cakes were not as good as she thought they were? She would take it personally because it was personal, very personal.

Acknowledging that those fears were there and that she would take things personally, Krissy also knew that she had more confidence than that, which was not in any way being arrogant. For she isn't egotistical at all; it is just that she really loves her cakes and desserts. The fear of people not liking them was not going to be enough to stop her. If anything was going to stand in her way, it would have been the practicality and the financial implications of setting up a business within the food industry.

Similarly, for Kevin there was also the financial fear of starting the business. He knew that it really would come down to being prepared to take a risk and roll the dice if he was to leave his job and throw his lot in with Krissy and start a bakery. Besides being the professional, focused and talented businessperson that he is, he can also be creative and think outside of the box or, in fact, remove the box altogether – a strength that would be a massive asset to the business, as it would be to any organisation. Equally, the fact that he is very employable and has a lot of professional experience under his belt, along with knowing that he is very good at what he does, meant he could always get a job in sales if it did not work out. This was the mindset he knew he would take into the business if he were to get involved. In addition, being the person he is, he knew that he would give it his all and do his best to see the business become the success it could be. Again, knowing that he could always get another job if it did not work out made it easier for him to get involved.

Having a family to support, and all the financial commitments and responsibilities that go with this, meant that there were a lot of financial constraints and fear holding them back. And they were reluctant to give up the security of the regular pay cheque that Kevin's job gave them, along with Krissy's income from her own work. Yet they also accepted that they were not getting any younger and if they were to go for it and set up their own business, then maybe their time had come. And that they could not allow the financial constraints and all the fear that this brought up to be enough to stop them.

Having accepted this was holding them back, they asked themselves whether it would be enough to stop them doing what they so wanted to do with their lives. The answer was a resounding 'no', for they also accepted that they were both very employable and would get jobs if their own business did not work out. They also accepted that they now wanted to do their own thing; that it would take a few years to build the business, so that meant having to do it now or maybe never!

Therefore, in October 2016, with a genuine sense of 'if not now, when then?' they made the brave decision to give it their best shot. Having made the decision to go for it, everything happened quickly from then on – just like it did for so many of the other storytellers in this book. Krissy initially worked full-time on setting up and running the new bakery, while Kevin stayed in his job, helping out when he could with deliveries, invoicing and general administration.

Then they got a big break by securing a major retail outlet as a customer. They knew that this contract really gave them something that they could build on and develop. This success, along with the fact that their bakery was getting busier and busier, also meant they knew they really were on to something. With this being the case, Kevin left his job and joined the business full-time.

Then, in February 2017, with the dream of providing customers with uncompromising cakes and desserts that bring joy to all who love to indulge themselves, they registered 'Take the Cake: Baking the World a Better Place' as a business in Ireland. Their business would lovingly bake authentic handmade desserts with no additives or preservatives, just like they had been made by Krissy's own mother, grandmother and great-grandmother before her.

As to now living the dream, well, are they? They tell me:

> When the two of us started working full-time in the business with no monthly wage packet coming in, that really was a scary time – and there's no other way to put it. Yet, even with this, there was also a genuine sense of relief about having decided to set up our own business and for then finally having made it happen.
>
> It is and has been physically, mentally and emotionally challenging and time-consuming. For more times than we can count it has been, like, 'What are we doing?' We have heard often how it takes time and hard work, and how full on it can be when working for yourself and setting up a business. This has been the case for us, and as we expected this, it has made it somewhat easier.

Regarding having spoken to anyone about their intentions to do what they did, they tell me, 'While there were no official meetings or anything like that, we told some friends and family about our intention to set up the business. Now, it wasn't about getting their advice or permission or anything like that, just more about letting them know what was happening, and people were supportive, very supportive and that has meant a lot to the two of us.'

Now, as to living the dream, the word 'gratification' comes to mind, for they believe they have created something completely new. In addition, they have made many people happy and they intend to continue making many more people happy with what they bake. That means a lot to them, it really does. What they also find gratifying is the fact that they are making something that is uniquely theirs, whereas in the past they attempted things that never quite came to be, which has been challenging. In what they are doing now, it feels like everything has come together for them at last. Therefore, yes, they believe they are living the dream, if for no other reason that they can now say: 'We made this happen: Take the Cake is ours and that is something that no one can ever take away from us.' So, what does the future hold for them? They tell me:

> Our goal now is to grow the business so that we can take a step back and not have to work all the time. We want to take a break from the kitchen, as well as not have to do all the deliveries and accounts ourselves. We want to grow 'Take the Cake' to a point where it takes on a life of its own and becomes the go-to brand in Ireland for cakes, giving us the time and financial resources to kick back a bit and enjoy the benefits of all our hard work.

With Krissy and Kevin's work ethic, the belief they have in themselves, their cakes and their business, there is every reason to believe that this will happen. When you meet and spend time with them, you leave with a sense that anything is possible when you bring lots of hard work, determination and passion to whatever it is you want to do.

Today, they are doing what they want to be doing, and they are still building as well as living the dream. They leave you in no doubt that 'Take the Cake' will be a massive success story. Just like Krissy and Kevin, all the storytellers in this book first had to figure out why they were born, and then go live it. Does any of this resonate with you?

Figuring out why they were born

Challenging as it was, the storytellers first needed to figure out why they were born and what work they needed to be doing. To do this, they:

- Started to question what the point of life was and more importantly what the point of their own life was;
- Began to believe they had to be worth more than the life they were living;
- Had a genuine sense of the life being lived was not working for them any more;
- Realised they no longer felt geared up for the life they were living;
- Understood they could not or did not want to go on living the life they were living;
- Believed there had to be more to life than the way they were living it;
- Asked what do they need to do to make their lives happier, better and more successful.

Having identified their strengths and figured out why they were born, they then wanted to go live their truth, as they now:

- No longer wanted to do what they were doing or live the way they had been living for the rest of their life;
- Wanted more than the life they were living;
- Believed the life they were living was just not good enough for them any longer;
- Had a genuine sense of wanting to live a life that felt right for them;
- Wanted to be more honest and true to themselves in their life and work;
- Knew they would be more resilient, persistent, self-confident and effective in all areas of their life for having pursued the life they were born to live;
- Understood and accepted that only they could get themselves out of the life they were no longer enjoying;
- Wanted to live a different life, a life better suited to them;
- Needed to wipe the slate clean and to begin anew, as they no longer wanted or were able to carry on with the life they were living;
- Had a strong desire to try new things;
- Were curious to know if it was possible to make a living from doing the work they truly wanted to be doing;
- Could no longer put off dedicating more time, energy, and commitment to making the life they truly wanted to be living become a reality;

- Knew that having figured out why they were born, they would now have to go live it if they were to have any life worth living at all;
- Accepted that it was up to them to do something about moving from a life they were not enjoying to one they could enjoy.

Likewise, many of them believed there is a real danger of letting life pass you by, as could have been the case for Amandine Passot Devine. Amandine was born in France and had been interested in journalism from a very young age. Having studied Economics and English at university in France in the late nineties and early noughties, she travelled to Ireland to study journalism part-time. In many ways, she had a great lifestyle as she was studying a subject she loved and had an income from a part-time job in administration, allowing her to enjoy a good standard of living for a student!

Unfortunately, her comfortable lifestyle was to get in the way of her dream of being a journalist after she finished her studies, for the simple reason that she was offered a full-time job in project management on a good salary. She took the job and continued to enjoy the lifestyle she had become accustomed to, building a career for herself and enjoying all the trappings that went with this. All of which meant that journalism would have to wait until another day. For the next sixteen years, she experienced milestones such as promotions at work, marriage, setting up home, children, redundancies, deaths and economic crashes. She lived through them all, learnt from them all and is so much the better for having come through them all.

Only, it was all to come to a head for her in December 2017. She still had a very well-paid job in project management and a great standard of living, only this was no longer enough to sustain her. It felt as if life were passing her by – and passing by fast. While she had had some very justifiable reasons in the past for not pursuing her dream of working in journalism, these no longer stacked up. For she had come to realise that each year she didn't pursue her dream was another year in which she wasn't doing what she wanted to be doing in her life; that at some stage, she would have to make the jump from the work she was doing to the work she had dreamt about doing when she was growing up in Paris all those years ago, if she was to be true to herself and her family. To do this, she had to become a person who contributed positively to society as a journalist. If this was ever going to happen, then it was time now to pursue her dream, for that was where she could make her biggest impact and be the best that she could be.

Having talked to her husband, Ciarán, the only other person she spoke to about leaving her job and going to live her dream was her friend Emer, with whom she had shared an apartment when first coming to Dublin. Emer was a little older than Amandine and just like a big sister to her, but when Amandine talked to her it was not as if she were looking for her advice. It was more a case of: 'I'm going to leave the profession and career that I've spent my life building to pursue a life as a journalist now!' She knew her friend would only confirm and support what she was now going to do, anyway.

In April 2018, at nearly forty years of age, Amandine handed in her notice and went to live her dream. A dream that started out by volunteering with a community radio station, where she researched and presented the news. She had not been volunteering there for long when the manager encouraged her to apply for a paid job at another community radio station. She did so – and got the job, which entailed researching, producing and presenting radio documentaries. It felt as if she had arrived! While the money was not great, the fact they were paying her to do what she had always dreamt of doing was a good enough start for her. She says: 'It felt great, for this was where I wanted to be. I loved it. It felt like I was walking on air, that this was my niche.'

Within only a year, an opportunity came up for Amandine to apply for a position with a national broadcaster. She submitted a successful application and they offered her a position in their pool of journalists, yet with no firm guarantees of jobs coming her way. Even if the work that she might initially have to undertake was not going to be the most demanding or challenging, that was perfectly okay for her at first. The position had the potential to take her to the highest level in broadcasting – and that was where she wanted to be. The fact that she would be getting paid once again to work in radio was just magical to her. Wanting to be available for the call when it would come, she handed in her notice and not long afterwards she was on her way again.

With one door closing in her work, it seems to be taking a long time before the next door opens for her. She's impatient for the call and questions herself. Maybe she had made a mistake and she should have stayed at the community radio station? It is a tough place to be, with a lot of rejection and having to deal with the uncertainty of where her next piece of work would come from. With work being quite slow, she is very grateful for the chance to make some radio documentaries and to write articles for publication as a freelancer. It's as if she is in a corridor, a place between where she was and where she now wants to be. She tells me:

> There are days when I sit here waiting, maybe applying for work and jobs that I know I will not get, or probably do not want anyway. The thing is, it gives me a sense that at least I am doing something. In addition, rejection is never that far away because I know I do not have the experience to get the jobs in the first place, even if I wanted them. Now I take some solace because I have the confidence to go for them, for the simple reason that I am pursuing my dream and nothing will stop me from achieving it. So, yes, this is what I want to do in my life and this can and often does come at a heavy price.

When Amandine finds herself sitting there and feeling a sense of rejection, or life just does not seem to be moving forward fast enough for her, it is a matter of changing the energy of her situation. To do this, she might get her hair done or meet a friend, or do something else that makes her feel good, like putting on her tracksuit and going for a run; for she knows that she cannot just sit there.

As to what the future holds for her, she tells me: 'First, it's all about having a structure as I pursue the dream of researching, producing and presenting documentaries for radio. Whether I get to do this as a paid employee or working freelance does not really matter, since this is how I now get to spend my time.' With the commitment, determination and energy she has to turn her dream into a reality, her dream of making radio documentaries will surely come true sooner rather than later.

Unlike many people, Amandine no longer risks letting life pass her by. Likewise, many of the storytellers got to a point where they were ready to play a hand in creating the life that they wanted to live – even if it was challenging. To survive was no longer enough, as they wanted to thrive in life; and they accepted that there was a timeline involved if this was ever going to happen. It became a case of getting going, for they truly understood that time and tide wait for no one. Something had to give if they wanted to come home to who they really were. In addition, this made them ask whether their life choices and decisions were comforting and nourishing their spirit, or whether these only offered temporary respite from having to deal with hard emotions, and were ultimately diminishing to their spirit. Were their choices leading to a life of genuine success, or did they leave them feeling empty? Having accepted that they no longer wanted to go on living the life they were living, they had to make a choice based on:

1. Do I sit here and spend the rest of my days complaining and whining about the life I am living? Or,

2. Do I get up, take responsibility for my life and go figure out what I am meant to be doing with it – and then go live it, whatever it takes?

Having answered 'no' to the first and 'yes' to the second, then it really came down to the storytellers creating a new future for themselves – and this can be the case for you too. Once you understand your true purpose in life:

- Clarity comes more quickly, which leads to your having more belief in the direction you want to bring to your life, which leads to your making faster decisions;
- When you make faster decisions, you'll often be the one who reaches a decision first and winds up making the best choices;

when you make the best choices, you have more opportunity for the best experiences.

Likewise, they know these truths:

- Living your life in accordance with why you were born is the straightest path to power and the ultimate source of personal strength, strength of belief and strength to persevere.
- The prescription for achieving extraordinary results lies in knowing what matters to you and then taking daily doses of action in alignment with this.
- Having clarity around the life you want to be living will help you when things just don't seem to be going your way.
- Living your life in accordance with what you really want to be doing will provide the ultimate glue to help you stick to the path you've set yourself towards and the life you desire.

- When what you are doing matches the life you are meant to be living, your days will feel harmonious, and the path you beat with your feet seems to match the sound in your head and heart.

- Living your life in accordance with whatever it is that you truly want to do is the most powerful approach of all and the happiest. For a sense of purpose, meaning and significance all make for a successful life.

The reasons the storytellers wanted to figure out why they were born and then go live it – myriad as they were – all stemmed from a single desire to become the author of their lives and the captain of their own ship. They had a longing to be true to themselves. To do the work that this entails, you have to rise and shine and commit to doing it. And you might just have to rock the boat too – and that is not always welcome! Could this be the case for you?

4. Don't Rock the Boat

But why you might just have to

So many things can stop people from living the life they truly want to live, the major one being that as humans we are psychologically, emotionally, cognitively and spiritually hardwired for belonging, love and connection. Connection, along with love and belonging (two expressions of connection), is why we are here, and for so many of us, it gives purpose and meaning to our lives. The only thing is, if you are to live the life you truly want to be living, then it might just mean having to back off and disengage from those around you, at least for a while anyway. Alternatively, it may even mean having to walk away from your old existence and those around you, as you set out on a new and better path for your life and work. But walking away from all that you know and the life you have been living can be tough. Tough for both you and those you are leaving behind. There may well be pain as you set out to live a new life, for as we are hardwired for connection, disconnection always causes us pain. What is happening now is that you are finding out who you really are as a person, not who you believe other people think you are or want you to be or become.

Now, it is no longer just a matter of fitting in. If you are to live your best life, it will have to be a life of belonging.

Fitting in and belonging are not the same thing. In fact, fitting in is one of the greatest barriers to belonging. Fitting in is about assessing a situation and becoming who you need to be so as to be accepted. Belonging does not require you to change who you are; it requires you to be who you are. That happens when you live a life that is true for you; for when you do, you become true to who you really are and get to show your true colours. Belonging is being where you want to be and where other people want you for who you are; unlike fitting in, which can mean being somewhere where you really want to be, yet they do not care about your presence either way.

Deciding to figure out and go live the life you were born to live can often cause significant concern and worry to those around you, particularly if it means having to disengage from or walk away from all you know. Others may well worry that you are 'giving up' on life. It can appear to the world as if you are running away from life, when in fact you are now running to life, whatever they may think.

What can often be harder still is if your culture, community or background uses a measuring stick of particular acquisitions and accomplishments to assess a person's worth. If this is the world you live in and the people with whom you associate, it will be a challenge to walk away from all this. Leaving the herd and safety of the life you know to live a new life is scary. This is why so few people do it.

There will be those who will rejoice with you as you go to live your new life. Yet many more will envy you for having the courage to do this. For many people, whether they admit it to themselves or not, there will be jealousy, lots of jealousy. Just like most of the storytellers in this book, you will need to start to care little for what others think of you and place yourself in the position of answering to no one, only to yourself. You will have to accept that what others think of you is none of your business.

Often, the fear of potential loneliness, rejection and ridicule can be too much for some. Better they do not rock the boat (a sailing term used by the captain to describe keeping things the way they are), as it seems much safer to do nothing and to stay living the life they have. Now, many of our storytellers talk of the loneliness they felt on going to pursue the life they were born to live. At the start, there was sometimes unbelievable loneliness and a genuine fear of never being part of anything again. For so many, this is often the point at which they falter. They struggle so much with the loneliness that they find it impossible to keep going and they return to their old life. The journey towards seeing their dream life become a reality seems just too much. The thing is, hard as it may be, this sort of loneliness is normal at the start of setting out to live your best life.

Now, this is not about pursuing your desires in a narcissistic sense. Whatever your goals, you will need to take into account, as best you can, your family, friends and relationships. But when you stop worrying about what everyone else thinks of you, there's no longer any need to try to be perfect all the time. Being concerned about what others think of you and striving to be perfect will no longer be enough to keep you from living the life you were born to live.

It can be tempting to wait until the 'perfect' moment and to be in the perfect position before attempting to live the life you truly want to enjoy. This is understandable, for so much importance is placed upon our being correct and being perfect. To be perfect in every sense, whether that's having the perfect teeth, figure, career, clothes, hair and partner, or the perfect life. The truth is that the idea of being perfect is really about trying to earn approval and being concerned about what others will think. It means being afraid of making mistakes, not meeting other people's or your own expectations – and the criticism that often goes with this.

If you strive to always get things right and achieve a sense of perfection, there is one sure outcome that this will have, and that is, it will crush your creativity. And being creative is exactly what you are doing when you set out to live your new life – for you truly are creating a new life. It is therefore often the pressure of perfection that stops people in their tracks from living their life to the full. If this is the case for you, please remember there's a lovely Egyptian proverb that says: 'A beautiful thing is never perfect.'

When you are living your life in accordance with showing your true colours, then that is a beautiful thing, imperfect as it may well be. Like the storytellers in these pages, you will often be your own greatest critic as you set out on your journey to your best life, so you don't need to take on board what others think of you on top of this. Change your attitude to a case of doing the right thing but not always about having to do everything right.

As well as perfectionism, there is the fear of failing and questions such as 'What if I don't create a paying job and/or make money out of what it is I am now going to do?' This too can and often does hold people back, as not only do they not want to fail but they don't want to be seen as a failure. The thing is, will these fears be strong enough to stop you from going forward with your life? Do you have what it takes or are you prepared to learn what it takes to deal with these fears and take the necessary steps to move your life forward? Remember that the best way to deal with any fear is to face it head-on – just like those telling their stories did.

With the untimely death of his father in 1985, this was to be the case for Adrian Haines, who at the age of only twenty-two took over the running of the family business. Based in the midlands of Ireland, it was a second-generation business that had now became a third generation one; and it consisted of a garage with petrol pumps, a small retail space and a large workshop where the staff repaired anything from chainsaws to motorbikes to cars, from tractors to buses. He tells me:

> This had not been the plan, Michael. Because of a truly inspirational teacher, my original intention was to study to become a teacher of religion or maybe even a Church of Ireland minister, only it was not to be.

It was not an easy start for him as the eighties were tough times to be running a business in Ireland. Interest rates were high and the business faced a big tax liability, which had built up over the years. A lot of debt had mounted up and there was no proper accounting system in place. Seven employees needed to be paid and there was not much work coming in. It was tough going – only, in July 1987, with the tax authorities paid and the probate finalised, the business was finally in his name. Adrian worked long hours and gradually built up the business, devoting particular attention to developing the bicycle business that his grandfather Sydney had started in 1898.

In 1990, Adrian met his future wife, Katherine, and they got married a couple of years later, going on to have two children, Ava and Mark. Then, in the late nineties, the business had expanded so much that it was time to look for new premises. Adrian set about planning a purpose-built 6000sq ft. site, with on-site parking and loading facilities as well as a storage yard. He explains:

> After all the planning and getting everything in place, we started building in July 2004 and were in by March 2005. I self-managed the project along with doing the day job and planning the move. It was a huge undertaking and stretched our resources. Not only did I have to fund the build but I had to stock it as well. The shop was ten times the size of the old premises. Eighteen months later, I had to borrow more money as I had underestimated the full cost of the build fit-out and stock. I remember taking out the last big business loan. The bank offered it for repayment over twenty-five years, but something made me say seventeen years to get it paid off and have it done by the time I turned fifty-five.

It was a decision he was to be grateful for later, as the stress of running the business 24/7 started to take its toll on his health. Then, in 2010, he attended a business course that was to have a profound effect on his life. During the course he set for himself the intention of having perfect health. Also, he made it clear to his son, Mark, that while he was there to support him, Mark was to plough his own furrow, as he did not want him to have to take over the business and have history repeat itself yet again! His daughter, Ava, had no desire to join the company. She had already become a teacher, like her mother.

With the constant challenge of trying to maintain good health, it was to take Adrian until 2015 to set up another company. It was the first step in creating his own individual identity separate from the inherited family business, and it was to be known as Haines of Birr Retail Ltd. Adrian continues:

> Michael, things were on the up as August 2018 was to be a great month for me. During Vintage Week, a local festival that has been running here for over fifty years, a customer who is a local auctioneer had his ride-on mower serviced at the garage. He called in on the Saturday after Vintage Week and enquired if I had ever thought of selling the family business. The potential buyer wished to remain anonymous for the moment.
>
> At the time, I did not give it much attention; only the idea took root, as earlier that year, I had put everything in order relating to the organisation of the business. Regardless of the offer, the thought of selling the business that had been in the family for three generations

had never really crossed my mind – only now it did and it was a thought that just wouldn't go away.

With our year-end being the 31 December, I gave serious thought to selling over the Christmas period. It was probably the first time in my life that I'd asked what was best for my family and me. Having discussed it with my family, I contacted the auctioneer and told him I might be interested in selling. He got back to me with a serious offer.

Likewise, the fact that my father had passed away at fifty-nine weighed heavily on me. The most important question I asked myself was, 'Is the business serving me?' The answer was clearly no, for I was running myself into the ground every year and felt that if I had to do another season, they would take me out in a box.

Other than his family, the only person Adrian confided in about these matters was a friend, who was a business adviser and whose wife had recently sold her own business. Taking his advice, Adrian engaged the services of a firm that specialised in business transfers. He explains:

> Having got over the third-generation family business stigma, I had everything ready to go from my end by the end of February. I met with the purchaser on the fourteenth of April, and we agreed a deal in principle and shook hands on it.

He adds:

At that moment, the relief was palpable. Also, I was finally taking a stand for my life.

The big focus then was to get the deal over the line and on 28 May contracts were signed, with Adrian finishing up in the business on 31 May. He says:

> I had set the intention and written on a piece of paper the amount I wanted for the business and had candles lighting over it from February until the deal completed. And the funny thing is, Michael, the price I was to get was the actual figure I had written.

He talks of the relief of being able to walk away from the business aged fifty-five, owing nothing to anyone, with a few quid in the bank, adding, 'Sure, didn't I only borrow from the bank for the seventeen years and not the twenty-five they wanted me to!' He also describes the many sleepless nights he had between deciding to sell the business and then finally selling it: the fear of losing his identity, as he had become the business and the business had become him, the possibility of having to make people redundant, and the end of Haines of Birr after so many years of very hard work rested heavily on his mind.

As to the future, he tells me:

> I will enjoy the newfound freedom that allows me to go for a walk or cycle when I feel like it. That having taken a stand for my own life, I am now the master of my destiny. A destiny that will see me build a new identity. That as a peacemaker and listener at heart, I will play to these strengths and do some further studies around

them, as I would like to bring together local business people with the intention of having us work together to offer a business or businesses that will serve the market, creating value and benefiting all involved.

Likewise, with my love for the outdoors, I will start a forest bathing guide course to assist people in reconnecting with themselves, trees and the natural world that surrounds us. It is all a work in progress. As I would also love to mentor young business people and share all that I have learnt from my time in business.

As you listen to Adrian talk and hear the passion in his voice, you just know that his future will be all about assisting others to deal with their fears and face them head-on, as he did himself in order to live his own truth. And he will show them how not to be afraid to rock the boat if you truly want to go and live the life you want to be living, doing the work you so want to be doing. Our storytellers understood that life is full of uncertainty and risk, and that our decisions and planning must take this into account when going forward to live the life we truly want to live. We must make sure to deal with the practical and financial implications of living the life we were born to live, aware that if we are scared our thinking won't be rational. The brain is extraordinary, and once we get rid of the fear, it usually finds an answer. And when we do, we will see how many other things start to fall into place.

All the same, as we saw earlier, many have the belief that they are too young or too old to change and this can often stop them from living the life they deserve. If this is the case for you, just remember Danny Range whom you read about at the start of the book. Later, you will meet Ann Keenaghan, who was older when she decided to change her life, but for now let's focus on Martin Deporres Wright. Martin was born in Dublin in 1951 and left school at seventeen, when he went to work for a National Irish Newspaper, just like his father before him. Having gained valuable experience in the advertising department while there, he went to work for an advertising agency in 1970. It was within this industry that he was to make his living for the next thirty-five years. During this time, he attended college, graduating in Advertising, Design and Art Direction, and worked in London, Beirut and Dubai. He became an award-winning art director and President of the Institute of Advertising.

In 2005, Martin set up his own advertising agency in Dublin. He tells me: 'I firmly believe that if you do the right thing in life, the right thing will happen to you. Setting up my own agency seemed like the right thing to do at that point in my life. It was as if this was the next challenge I had to respond to professionally if I was to continue to create great content and keep doing superb work.' His agency went on to do fantastic work and became in a brief period of time one of the most creative agencies in the country, winning national newspaper awards along the way.

It was to all change in 2009 because of the economic crash in Ireland. Work stopped coming in, yet the bills did not. It felt as if Martin and his team might never work again and as he was now fifty-eight years of age, it was a genuine challenge not to think his days in advertising were over. It proved to be a difficult, stressful and challenging time, both professionally and personally. Then, in 2011, he got a call from Dubai, inviting him to set up and lead a new advertising team in an agency there. It was the very challenge and opportunity he had been hoping would come his way. Having talked it through with his wife, Bernadette, and gaining her support, he based himself in Dubai and commuted from his home in Dublin. Two years later and having completed the work sooner than expected, he moved back home. While in his sixties, he was not ready to ease up just yet. He started working freelance within the advertising industry.

It was while working as a freelancer that he rediscovered his love of painting and came to know the enjoyment and pleasure of being a sculptor. At home one day, he stumbled across some old paints, so he went out and bought a roll of paper just like those used in the printing world. As the paint touched the paper, he heard himself say, 'Holy shit, this is so relaxing and enjoyable!' Right there and then, he had an overwhelming sense of happiness as he painted.

Not long afterwards, he found himself in the builder's yard next door, which been derelict for many years. He met the owner, who was more than happy to give him permission to use a cabin made from a shipping container for a studio, if he was prepared to clean it out first, as it had not been in use since the recession. Martin was happy to do so. Having cleaned it out, he then had his own studio, which allowed him to work on bigger projects and pieces of art than it would have been possible for him to do at home.

Walking to the studio one day, Martin tripped over a roll of old Richmond felt (a kind of roofing material) in the builder's yard. With the owner's permission, he took the roll back to the studio, rolled it out flat and discovered there were all these parallel lines on it because it had been lying there so long. As he painted one line and then the next line with a different colour, they blended into each other – and he knew in that moment he was on his way to establishing a new career for himself as an artist, for there was a real feeling of being reborn which was something he wanted to pursue.

While still making himself available to carry out freelance work within the advertising industry, it was possible for him now to become an abstract painter and sculptor as well. This has been the case for him ever since: while he is available for freelance work, he is now spending more and more of his time as a professional painter and sculptor. As to getting to live his passion – the dream, so to speak – and do what he was born to do, the answer is a resounding 'yes'; as he tells me:

> I truly felt very fortunate and privileged to have entered an industry and have a career that allowed me to address my creativity as I am now getting to do. I never fell out with the alarm clock during my days working in advertising and it is the same today, as I get to pursue my passion and love of all things creative as a professional painter and sculptor. To be doing so at this stage of my life is just brilliant, and something for which I am so very grateful.

After only a brief period of time as a painter and sculptor, Martin is now travelling the world and exhibiting his work both nationally and internationally. This allows him to make his creative and artistic contribution to the world, just as he did so successfully during his advertising career. As to what he would love to see happen next, well, that is simple, as he explains:

> I want to continue making my unique contribution to the arts, as I was able to do so for so many years within the advertising world. As to doing the next right thing, I will just stay open to the universe and let that bring me to where I need to go. Yes, this will mean there will be a lot that I will have to do – and this has me excited for the new decade and decades ahead. I maintain my sense of gratitude and privilege in being able to produce artwork and stay ever grateful to my wife, Bernadette, who I married in 1977, and to our children and grandchildren.

So, Martin is making comprehensive plans for the future, only he is quick to remind me: 'While I'm making plans, I'm not planning the outcome! I will continue to keep taking the next right step, despite how difficult this can appear to be. Knowing that when I do, it keeps bringing me towards where my work and life need to be going.'

His story, like those of so many of the storytellers, shows that the creative impulse can often improve with time and experience. This could be because of our accumulated memories, as older adults are often good at connecting the dots. This sort of wisdom can lead to mature people being very innovative. Maybe it is because of this wisdom and the lessons learnt from life that today we are seeing greater numbers of older adults becoming entrepreneurs. In addition, the more we recognise and support them in this, the more they will express this form of creativity for the betterment of us all. All the same, while the creative impulse can often improve with time and experience, this should not be an excuse to wait to get going!

If, like Martin, it is possible for you to move seamlessly from the work and life you are living to the work and life you want, that's great. If this is not possible, then maybe it is still possible for you to create a new job to make the most of your strengths in the area in which you already work, or there may well be another profession out there that calls for your strengths. It might just be a combination of both, where everyone gets to win. This was the case for Medbh Boyle, who was educated in one of Ireland's first multi-denominational schools in the 1980s. This was to lead to her having a fascination for understanding different religions and cultures, as well as developing a lifelong interest and desire for spiritual exploration.

Having completed school in 1999, Medbh went to university to do an arts degree, only to leave in 2001, as it just was not for her. She was then to have several jobs, which she loved as they led to her facilitating drama and arts workshops with teenagers in youth and community services. This in turn had her return to college and graduate in 2008 with a diploma in Drama. Throughout all this time, she continued to find solace in spiritual texts, retreats and meditation. In 2009, she integrated all the benefits she received from meditation and personal development into training to be a life coach for her youth and community work. Her wish to up-skill, along with her commitment to helping young people, had her return to university in 2012, aged thirty-one.

After graduating with a first-class honour's degree in Applied Social Sciences in 2015, Medbh went back to working full-time as a youth worker. Then, in 2016, her fascination for different religions and cultures, including Buddhist meditation and nature-based shamanic practices, saw her commute to London from Dublin to train as and then be ordained as a non-denominational OneSpirit interfaith minister in 2018. She tells me:

> As my own spiritual capacity grew, I realised that more and more people were looking for a bit of what I had – a sense of connection, calm, access to meaning, ritual, and access to communities of support and practice. This, along with the sadness of seeing Irish society become so competitive and caught up in consumerism, with a need now more than ever for more 'soulful living', acted as a catalyst for me studying to become an ordained interfaith minister. All of my previous training in theatre, community and group work, life coaching and my personal journey equipped me with an excellent skill set for the work of spiritual ministry.
>
> Yet, even with all that going for me, it still took great dedication to keep up with the intensive training and having to travel back and forth to London. Likewise, not knowing how I would afford it financially, let alone knowing where it would lead me work wise, were enormous challenges. Another challenge was I would need to be very brave when describing what and why I

was doing it, for the Church and religion is territory that can often be emotionally charged for people.

She originally told only her friends Sarah and Adrienne of her intention to train as an interfaith minister. As her vocation progressed and become a reality, she told more friends and family, expecting them to think she was mad! Which thankfully was not the case, although it can often be for many people setting out on a new and very different path in life. In fact, everyone thought it was a perfect fit for her, and some of them expressed a need for a more alternative spiritual ministry in their own lives and community just like the one she now intended to offer.

As for living the dream and following her passion, she says: 'Yes, absolutely, I have followed my passions in life bit by bit, and that has led me to a dream which unfolded as I took the necessary steps to move my life forward – and this has made all the difference.'

When it comes to what the future holds for her, she tells me: 'I know the future is all about taking responsibility for myself, and that means being vulnerable. Therefore, I have to be strong enough within myself to be of service to others regardless of their age or the circumstances. I will continue to follow my passions, use my strengths and allow synchronicity to play its part as it has done in bringing me to where I am now in my life and work.'

She will continue working part-time as a youth worker, doing a job that she loves, is passionate about and committed to. The rest of the time will be dedicated to her ministry, holding ceremonies, spaces and conversations. All the while assisting people to access their own sense of spirituality and become authorities over their own soulful lives. It is also her intention to combine her interfaith training with her youth work to develop rites of passages for young people. She explains: 'It really is as if I have the best of both worlds. As I get to do work, which allows me to use my strengths and also have time to do my interfaith ministry as a priestess [as she refers to herself]. I also now see my mission as creating a very welcome and welcoming space for every young person who arrives into this country wanting to make it their new home.' Having met and spent time with her, you just know that she will get to do all this and more as she lives what she was born to do.

Now, what if you cannot stay in your job and earn an income? This is the case for a lot of people who have figured out why they were born and the work they now want to do. Many of them face the challenge of walking away from a career they may well have built up over many years. If this is the case for you too, then you may well be looking at the creation of an entirely new service or profession, and starting your own business and new way of life. The financial insecurity of having to leave your job and set up your own business or make a living differently can be daunting. It can be too much for some and stops them from pursuing the life they want to be living. For even if you do know what you want to do, there can be no guarantee of translating it into successfully making a living. This and the following major reasons often stop people from living the life they are meant to be living; we have already looked at aspects of these but let's revisit them now:

- The concern and upset that can be involved in giving up the life they are living may be too much for some people.

- The idea of leaving the herd and safety of the life they know might be too scary.

- The worry of dealing with rejection and ridicule should they fail, and being seen as a failure, can be too daunting.

- Waiting till the perfect moment or to be in a perfect position – which never comes – before pursuing the life they truly want to be living.

- Lack of self-belief that they are good enough and deserve to be living the life they were born to live.

- Being unwilling to make mistakes and not meeting other peoples' or their own expectations, and the challenge of dealing with the criticism that may come with this.

- The struggle to deal with the often unbelievable loneliness, along with the genuine fear of never being part of anything ever again, might just make some people go back to their old life.

Do you believe any of these would apply to you? If so, will these challenges be enough to stop you from doing now what you really want to be doing with your life?

Alternatively, is it a case of staying where you are and not rocking the boat? Or are you willing to stand out from the crowd, rock the boat and go live the life you were born to live? If so, are you prepared to give up the life you have been living and deal with all the challenges that may possibly come with this? And to deal with and overcome the often added pressure from others to stay where you are and not risk possibly losing the life and career that you have worked so hard to build up? Can you ignore the demands placed on you to conform and stick with what you know, aware that to do otherwise might just mean others think you have gone mad?

In spite all of this, are you ready to go for it, knowing that occasionally, just like so many of those here, you may have to go against the grain and not accept how society would have you play it safe and not rock the boat? If so, for you it may be a case – as it was for so many of our storytellers – of cracking on in pursuit of the life you were born to live.

5. Cracking On

All you have is now

How do you make the life you were born to live become an everyday reality for you?

Well, at the start you may well need to keep your decision to pursue it to yourself, just like so many of our storytellers did, until you are ready to face those around you. Maybe tell your partner and possibly one or two trusted souls, yet possibly do not mention it even to your extended family; for your family and friends will likely have genuine concerns about how you will now make a living. It may even be the case that if you tell colleagues and friends, they will criticise you for walking away from the career you have built, which might have you starting to question yourself at the precise moment you are about to take the next step to go live the life you really want to be living. Listening to them may only heighten your own concerns, thoughts and fears at this precious and delicate time for you.

When you need to be building up your self-belief to go forward with your life, you might not be met with any positive responses. In fact, all you might receive are the inner fears and concerns of others, with their fears and concerns projected onto you. If this becomes the case, then as our storytellers did, you will need to accept it really is your responsibility alone to decide whether to go live this new life of yours or not.

As we have seen, it might even be the case that the people surrounding you will be jealous of your success for having figured out why you were born, let alone the fact that you now intend to go live your truth. The truth of what you are now about to do could very likely make those around you feel uncomfortable. It could remind them how often they have not followed their own dreams. Therefore, you may need to withdraw and keep your plans to yourself until you act on them.

Having made the decision to pursue the life you truly want to be living, it is then all about cracking on (a sailing expression, which means to get moving or hurry up) for, as we know, time and tide wait for no one. This was certainly the case for Sharon Rossignuolo, who is a component and confident communicator today, yet this has not always been the case. Growing up on a farm in the West of Ireland in the 1980s, she was painfully shy and would go red every time she had to speak up in class, for as she tells me: 'My communication skills weren't the best and being confident wasn't something that would have been high up on the radar for me.' Having finished school, she went to university, studying in her own words, 'English for the power of words and History for the power of adventure and stories of courageous people who changed the world.'

After finishing university, Sharon moved to Dublin to teach for six months. She then travelled to Turin, Italy, where – having qualified as a TEFL teacher – she taught

English as a foreign language. Despite being just twenty-one-years-old, she taught English to business owners, corporate professionals, university students, lawyers, international trainers and antique dealers. It was there she learnt the importance of communicating clearly, and to truly appreciate diversity and inclusion. Only, having gone abroad with all guns blazing, she quickly grew homesick and bored. At the same time, she saw people a lot older than her doing the same sort of work for the same pay as her. She knew this was not the career and life for her.

So, sixteen months later she was back in Dublin, working for a telecommunications company. It was here that she was to set out on her leadership path and earn a reputation as someone with a genuine passion for people and achieving results, even winning the 'Empathy Champion' and 'Hero Awards'. Then, a little over seven years later, she went to work in the financial services sector, which brought her into a completely new industry. After five years, it was time for her to move on once again and she went to work for a multinational e-commerce corporation. As the leader of multicultural, multifunctional teams, she was awarded the title of Outstanding Manager of the Year, along with receiving various other awards for innovation and team engagement.

The only trouble was that while she was very successful at her job, she had taken the focus off her own health and wellbeing. She knew that if she were to continue working at the pace she had set for herself, while it would bring her great recognition and rewards at work, the price would be at the cost of her health, along with having very little quality time with her family. It was a price she was not prepared to pay any longer. After talking it through with her husband, Marco, who was 100 per cent supportive of her, she handed in her notice. She intended to set up her own business, which she believed would allow her to determine her own boundaries and decide how much time, effort and energy she wanted to dedicate to her working life. She also felt ready for another adventure where she could make her next big impact and difference.

Regarding losing a guaranteed income, she knew there would be implications. At the same time, once she had handed in her notice there would no longer be any need to spend money on expensive weekends away or other luxuries to compensate for all the things she and her loved ones did not get to do as a family when she was working. And while expensive, these luxuries were not that enjoyable. They often just involved more time away from home while trying to make up for the time she already spent away from there, caught up in the rat race. Okay, she did not know what lay ahead, saying: 'It may have been more stupidity than anything else, only I really did not have any fear because I had a little business idea that I wanted to pursue. I thought everything would be fine. In fact, at the time I could not have been happier.'

So, in October 2014, having handed in her notice, and not knowing what lay ahead, let alone how things would work out, Sharon took the following three months off. She says: 'It was like a honeymoon period, with such a sense of freedom. It was magical, having free time and not having to run around and juggle everything. I was just so happy to drop our two kids off to school. I remember noticing the flowers and nature and saying hello to people as they passed by.'

After her three months off, Sharon started her own entrepreneurial adventure by setting up her first business, which was based on helping international non-native English-speaking professionals and business owners to become more accurate and effective in communicating. Only, she was to make all the rookie mistakes of a new entrepreneur, telling me, 'Of going to step ten before doing step one. It was a saturated market with very little money to be made.'

After nearly two years, in December 2016 it was time to move on, taking with her once again the hard-earned lessons she'd learnt. Based on her experience, and understanding the extra hurdles that women, particularly female entrepreneurs, have to climb over in order to push themselves and their companies forward, Sharon wanted to make a difference by setting up a business that responded to this. She also knew that it was rarely about competence and much more about the confidence that women needed to succeed as entrepreneurs and business leaders. She could play her part in seeing them succeed at every level. With all of this in mind, she is now living her purpose by both making a difference and earning a living through empowering people – especially women – to be better leaders and more successful business owners and entrepreneurs. This work also has her managing the Fingal Enterprising Women Network, which is all about providing learning and networking opportunities for women in business and enterprise. When she's not doing this, you will find Sharon at home with her husband and their two daughters.

As to what the future holds for Sharon, that is simple. Like so many of our storytellers, she will tell you:

> My life and work to date have not been in a straight line. There have been many difficulties, challenges faced and overcome, along with very many lonely moments – and particularly so since going to work for myself.
>
> Sometimes it would have been easier and simpler to get a 9 to 5 job. Only I knew that was not the way forward for me. The work I am doing is the work I am passionate about doing. This is the right place for me at this time in my life. Therefore, I've given no real thought at all to stopping and getting a 9 to 5 job.
>
> Being so passionate about wanting to see women succeed as leaders and entrepreneurs will have me continue this journey. I am on a journey of empowering people to reach their full potential in business and as leaders through confidence-building and improved communication skills and networking. For this is where I believe I can make my biggest impact and difference.
>
> Likewise, if it ever gets to a point that I'm not enjoying what I am doing or making a positive difference, and cannot make the impact that I want to be making for the good of all people – in particular the people around me – then I'll move on to something else.

Given how passionate Sharon is to see women succeed, you know she won't be going anywhere soon, for she's so good at what she does and loves what she does too much. Having chosen to go live the life you truly want to be living, just like Sharon did, the challenge then is to bridge the gap between the life you are living and the life you want to be living. The only way of bridging that gap is to take the necessary action to make change happen. Because action trumps everything else.

In life, however, you cannot control everything – and it is the same with this new life of yours, so do not look too far ahead. Focus on the things in front of you and get them done – and done well. Those things you cannot control, let them go and put them out there into the universe, so to speak. Personally, I choose to ask God for help. Start by taking the first small step in front of you to bridge the gap from where you are to where you want your life and work to be. This baby step will see you make the first move towards directing your life to where you want to it to be.

What happens, then, if it all gets too challenging for you? Well, if it does, you have a choice to either fold or focus. To fold and give up – or to stay focused on the life you want to be living and to keep going for it. Regardless of how tough it may get (particularly at the start), remain hopeful for a better future, a brighter future, for when you are hopeful you are still in the game. When you have hope, you always have a chance regardless of what life is throwing at you.

What happens, then, if it all goes belly up? Then, as for many of our storytellers, you too will have to start over once more. Yet continue to remain hopeful and be open to fresh opportunities, knowing that if you stay the course, things will work out – and if it is not working out, then you just have not finished yet. Understand and accept that, like our storytellers, you too have the intuition and inner skills you need to go live a new life – regardless of what life throws at you. Tap into the very same qualities and skills that you used in the first place to figure out why you were born. Appreciate the fact that you have had to deal with and overcome many challenges in your life to date, and know that you will once again come through and deal with all challenges placed before you in pursuit of the life you truly want to be living.

Equally, when things are going your way, people will tell you to keep things in perspective – and that is fair enough. Particularly when you are starting out, they may see your pursuit of your new life as being an all-encompassing quest and tell you that it is all about finding balance and living a balanced lifestyle. Now remember, balance is an idea. As they might say in Ireland, it is a grand idea. Only it is not a very practical one. If you want to live your best life, balance will rarely exist. For it is a very idealistic concept and not at all realistic.

Like the accomplishment of all extraordinary results, what you are trying to achieve will often mean having to give it your all in pursuit of having it all. You may have to give all your time to achieve what now matters most to you to see it become a reality. This being the case, a balanced lifestyle may be impossible as you dedicate yourself to living the life you were born to live.

If you are told you are out of balance or you feel this might be the case for you, it usually means that other things that matter are not getting attention. The fact is that when you truly do what is most important to you, some things won't get done or receive attention. This is a necessary trade-off for the achievement of extraordinary results, just like the achievement of the life you truly want to be living, which will often require your total focus and energy on that and that alone.

There will also be a lot of fear, both real and perceived, as you take the steps to bring your life forward. Like we have already seen, the fear never goes away fully. Likewise, this can be a time of big changes. And with change, what people fear most of all is loss. This could be the loss of the old life they had been living and all the security and safety that went with that. As you move from the life you are living to the life you want to live, there may well be a sense of loss for all that you are now leaving behind. When dealing with and overcoming this sense of loss, our storytellers were first of all grateful for the life they had lived. They acknowledged what they were losing and leaving behind as they let go of their old life. They accepted that they were going through this to experience the better life that lay ahead. As they took steps to move forward, they stayed focused on the life they wanted to live, knowing that this is a great way to deal with fear.

Is it now time for you to just go for it? To muster up the courage to take that leap from the life you are living towards the life you really want to be living? Are you now ready to embrace the support of your family, friends and colleagues if it is there and to go for it – regardless of the challenges you have to face? Regardless of whatever support you may or may not have, are you now ready to take the action to move your life forward as you focus on the life you want to be living and not on the life that you are leaving behind?

Those telling their stories here went for it, while accepting there was no guarantee of how it was all going to work out for them. Yet the hope was there that everything would all work out just right for them, as it will for you. They accepted that it would be challenging, particularly so at the start. It may even be an ongoing challenge or you may even fail. If there is such a thing as failure, and if you do fail, know that you will come back from this stronger.

Regardless of the circumstances that they faced, when you meet our storytellers you just know you are meeting a group of self-leaders who are setting the course of how they live their lives. They are determined, focused and are playing to their strengths in ways that allow them to keep moving forward in pursuit of the life they want to be living. You, like them, can now muster up the courage to take that leap of faith from the life you are living to the life you want to live. At the same time, you will need to accept that having made the brave decision to go live that new life of yours, it might just take a while to see it become a reality. This was the case for so many of those telling their stories here and if this proves to be the case for you, then take heart from Barry Kirwan's story.

As Barry was born into a very well-known and successful musical family in County Tyrone, it was no wonder that he had showbiz aspirations from a very early age. Having finished school and showing a particular passion for drumming, he went to London to study at Drumtech, part of the British and Irish Modern Music Institute (BIMM) schools. Shortly after finishing college, he joined his father Dominic's band as the drummer and provided backing vocals for over four years. Constantly growing as a musician, he left the band in September 2010 and lived with his brother Colm in Nashville, the music capital of the USA.

Then, as January 2011 came to a close, Barry started working with Ireland's princess of country music, Lisa McHugh, and performed with her until September 2011. At this point, he became the drummer and backing vocalist for the hit recording artist Derek Ryan. During his four and a half years working with Derek Ryan's band, Barry toured all around Ireland, the UK and Australia. With every show in every city, his desires became more apparent, and in February 2016, at the age of thirty, he left the band to pursue his own dream of a solo career in the Irish country music scene. This included touring with his father as the support act on the 'Here For A Good Time' tour in the UK and Ireland. It proved to be an excellent platform on which to prepare for his own live shows that summer.

That year Barry also released his first solo single, 'Keep It In The Middle Of the Road', from his debut studio album. The song shot to the number one spot on the Irish iTunes country chart and was number two in the UK iTunes Country chart. Barry went on to be nominated for 'Newcomer of the Year' at the 2016 RTE Irish Country Music Awards – foretelling the successful career this rising star was to have and how he was to take the Irish country scene by storm.

Having spent years building his career in country music and given all the hard work he had done, it was no wonder Barry felt that 2020 was going to be his year. Only it didn't turn out to be the case, for it was to all fall apart as COVID-19 became a major part of all our lives. Almost immediately, he lost his chance to tour Scotland and England with his dad, which amounted to nearly fifty gigs. He tells me:

> The more the lockdowns went on and things got shut down, more and more gigs were being cancelled – and not only in 2020 but for the following year as well. With no money coming in and with a family to support, I had to get a job; I just needed the money. I mean, I've worked from the age of thirteen, from when I was a paperboy. It is just in my nature to work. So yes, I needed to work to earn some money, only I also needed to work for my own sanity.

So, dealing with the reality of his situation and not letting his ego get in the way, he goes and gets a job. He says:

> I had a big year ahead and then the next thing is I'm standing outside a supermarket in Omagh [where he's from] sanitising trolleys after customers had used them. It felt a little awkward at the start, as people would have associated me with being on the stage; only, you know, people were great. It was as if they knew I had a family, so why would I not be out there trying to earn a living? With that in mind, it was as if they had a certain regard for me and what it was I was doing, so the awkwardness did not last. Then the more I settled in, the more I liked

it. While I meant it to be temporary, I just knew the longer the pandemic went on, there would be a need to get something more secure, as the music would not come back anytime soon.

With this in mind, he was determined not to let the fact that he'd never written up a CV or had much experience with job interviews stand in his way. He saw a more secure job in a different supermarket with regular hours and a guaranteed income: 'I talked it through with Michelle [his partner], who was so supportive and I didn't talk to anyone else – for after that I really did not care what anyone else thought.' He applied for the job and got it. As he says himself:

> It is what it is. While this may not have been part of my original plan, I would not sit around feeling sorry for myself and giving out about the state of the world. For while things have not gone the way I would have hoped for, I really feel optimistic about the future. So I am getting on with my life and making the most of it. In fact, I am enjoying the work I now do – and above all else I am very grateful for it.

Regarding the future, he tells me, 'The music will come back and that is what I love to do. So, yes, I will return to it, when it is safe to do so. In the meantime, we just have to ride this storm out, so I will keep recording and doing live sessions on Facebook to keep my artistic side ticking over.'

Sometimes, what might seem to be going against you might in fact end up going for you – as was the case for

Barry. For while the pandemic might initially have gone against him, he has made the most of it. He finishes by telling me:

> While music is my first love, I am enjoying the job and would love to stay working there and do the music when it returns. When you are touring, there is a lot of time off and I have discussed this with management, who have all been great. So, yes, it would be great to get to do the music, stay working there and have a regular income. The music business can be very busy and at other times very quiet, so you have to work your money out over the year – and the job would be a great help with this.
>
> Likewise, I will keep on making the most of the situation we now find ourselves in. For I got to make an album during this time with a good friend of mine, which has been something that I would never have had the chance to do before. And being able to keep it local and give them the business was also great, and that too is something for which I am very grateful.

You just know that with the talent Barry has, the manner in which he carries himself so humbly and his strong work ethic, neither this setback nor any other setback will be enough to stop him from doing what he truly wants to be doing with his life and work.

Often, as was the case for Barry, things may not just seem to go your way as you begin to live out the reason why you were born, and particularly so at the start of your journey. Many of our storytellers talk of the periods of transition that occurred as they moved into their new lives. These periods acted like a corridor between the life they had been living to the life they now wanted to live, acting almost like a timeout period between the two and an opportunity to give themselves the time to come to terms with why they were born, let go of their old life and figure out the next step they had to take. This period can often be seen as a time where to the outside world it appears as if you are being selfish, or indeed have gone backwards in your life and career. Because this time is all about you, it is all-consuming. It is a time of turning inward as you now come to accept that you and you alone have to decide how best you can now bring your life forward to where you want it to be.

This can often mean having to disengage from others – if not physically, certainly emotionally and psychologically. It is important to use this time to deal with and let go of the past, and decide how best to move forward and to build up the energy and courage to take the next step in bringing your life and work to where you want them to be. The storytellers will tell you this can and often is a tough place in which to find yourself. Yet they will also tell you that it was as if this was exactly where they needed to be in their life at that point.

When the time comes for you to leave the corridor, it may mean you have to physically move from one place to another in pursuit of the life for which you were born. This was the case for Ann Keenaghan, who I mentioned briefly earlier. Ann grew up in a family that ran a business in Co. Donegal in the north-west of Ireland. The business included a B&B, souvenir shop and caravan park, and might just have been the reason why Ann chose to study business too, having completed her leaving certificate in 1972 aged seventeen.

The following year, with her studies successfully completed, Ann's friend Lily applied for a position in the bank, so Ann did too. She got the job, and at the age of eighteen started working for the bank in Co. Cavan, which meant moving from her home town. It was there she was to meet her now ex-husband, whom she married at the age of twenty-one. They were to have three children by the time she was thirty. Her common sense, calm demeanour and magnificent gift for getting on with people were to see her promoted at a young age to acting Assistant Manager in the bank. Then, in 1989, she and her family emigrated. She explains:

> Having emigrated to Australia, while my ex-husband hoped to settle there, I always felt we would be back within two years. Sometimes dreams don't always turn out to be what they seem. We had sold our house and had to start over again, being down a lot of money with five airfares and moving our possessions back and forth. I got temporary work back in the bank within three weeks of having returned, at a lower rate of pay. Thankfully, the temporary contracts kept coming for the next four years. During this time, we purchased a house again, taking out a mortgage and starting over. The children were amazing in how they dealt with all the upheaval. They have always brought me great joy in my life.

As her children got older, Ann had time to work voluntarily on the board of directors for the local credit union. The chairperson called her one evening to ask if she would go to a meeting about the government's intention to fund a new free money advice and budgeting service (MABS), which was being set up to support local communities. Saying yes, Ann went to the meeting to hear that such a service was being set up in Cavan and they were forming a local management committee to make this happen. Once set up, their first task would be to employ a coordinator. Her first thought on hearing this was: 'I would love that job.' Therefore, she didn't volunteer to be on the committee, but applied for the job of coordinator and was successful.

She took to the job straight away and loved it from day one. When her marriage ended in 2004 after twenty-seven years, she was suffering badly with back pain and went for her first back massage. Dolores, the woman she went to, had also studied many other therapies over the years and had a background in the bank too. Ann tells me: 'We connected immediately and Dolores offered me healing, which I was happy to accept and could immediately sense subtle changes in my body.'

On relating her experience of the healing to Dolores, Dolores told Ann she would be naturally good at turning in to energy healing herself. Ann initially laughed at this, only when she went to see a kinesiologist she was told the same thing. With her interest spiked, she booked into a one-day basic training course on Integrated Energy Therapy (IET). She says, 'Having gone, I absolutely loved it. Over the coming years, I attended many more courses, including training as a kinesiologist and integrated energy therapist and instructor/trainer, and I also studied herbal remedies. All of which opened up a whole new path in my life that has led me to where I am now.'

She started working a four-day week in MABS in 2005, giving her more time to share all that she was now learning with individuals and groups. Then, while staying with her daughter Sinead, who was living and studying in Galway, she visited Connemara and the craft village in Spiddal. She says:

> As I sat outside a cafe there, I was looking across the ocean and found the coastline enchanting. I had grown up with beautiful scenery, but this was different. I became aware later that I was looking at the Burren and know now that I was being drawn by its energy.
>
> Then, while staying in a B&B in Spiddal, I felt 'at home'. I told the owner, Barbara, that I could live there right now with just the bag I had with me. She laughed and said an artist had booked in for a week one summer and stayed until he died fourteen years later.

Much as she wanted to move to Spiddal, Ann never saw it as a possibility at that time and forgot about it once she was back home in Cavan. The idea of taking out a mortgage and all that goes with that meant it was not possible for her to just give up her job and move there. With this in mind, her intention was to work part-time until her retirement and to provide a healing service during the rest of the time. Only, in 2009 she had a car accident and could not work in MABS or provide any of her healing work for five months. She could not look at TV or a computer screen, be on a phone for any length of time or be around people, as every noise seemed amplified for her.

Having eventually gone back to work in MABS, she found it a genuine struggle to focus on facts, figures and to manage the office. Yet this was not the case for her healing work, as she seemed to be even more tuned in to people's energies – and in particular their emotional pain. As a child, she would often sense how people were feeling, and this became magnified then. Having struggled on for a year and a half to work two days a week in MABS, she tells me: 'Then one day I just knew I had to leave and start a healing practice full-time. I never questioned it; I just knew.'

Not wanting to create any fuss, she told only family and close friends before handing in her notice and leaving her job in 2010. She then went to stay for six weeks with her son Ruairí, who was living just outside Galway, before renting a place herself in Spiddal. She says:

> I always knew Spiddal was the right place for me when I went to move there. All these years later, the view across the sea to the Burren has lost none of its enchantment.
>
> Now, in other ways it has not been the easiest of journeys. My house did not sell, and then the effects of the recession set in. The value of the house dropped to under a quarter of its original value, and the equity that had been there disappeared. The equity that was to buy me a smaller house in Spiddal. Yet there has been so much other magic along the way. Like when I was flying

to China to visit my son Seán Óg, I sat beside a Chinese qi gong master (who is also a Chinese doctor) on the plane. It has been my pleasure many times since to have hosted him here in Connemara to teach qi gong and Taoist meditation.

As to what the future holds for her, she tells me: 'I honestly don't know. Only I am looking forward to more magic, surprises and wonderful experiences along the way. I plan to teach more workshops in IET, qi gong and meditation. To enjoy my family and friends. Have more fun. Travel and to continue spreading love and light in the world.'

While Ann might tell us that she doesn't know what the future holds for her, we can be sure of one thing: that she, like the rest of those telling their stories here, will keep following the right tack that will see her stay on course to live the life she truly wants to be living.

6. The Right Tack

Staying on it

Figuring out why you were born is one thing. To then go live it is another, as it requires tremendous commitment, discipline and sometimes great courage to take the action needed to see the new life you desire become a reality. This is why living the life you are meant to be living is often not for the faint-hearted. Sticking with what you know to be right for you, when the odds can and often will be against you, will take great determination. Along with hard work, lots of hard work… every single day. While it may not have been easy, our storytellers will tell you it really is worth it. For as tough as it can be, they would not have had it any other way. Having stuck with it, they came to understand and accept that only by being true to themselves could they get to live the life for which they were born.

Now, as you move from the life you are living to the life you want, things might not always go the way you would like them to. As we have seen, this can be particularly so at the start and you may have doubts as to whether or not this is the life you are meant to be living. What, then, if this is the case for you? How will you know that you are living the life you were born to live?

It is simple. For regardless of what is going on in your life, if you can answer 'yes' to any or all of the following questions, you are on the right tack (a sailing term explaining that you are proceeding satisfactorily and therefore also following the correct line of reasoning) to living the life you were born to live:

- ✔ Is the life you are leaving behind just not a life that you want to live anymore? Many of the storytellers will attest to the fact that while the living out of their new life was often challenging and unpredictable, it was better than the life they left behind. Tempting as it may have been at the difficult times, they knew they could not go back to their old life. For to do so would have meant not being true to themselves and the person they wanted to be and the life they now wanted to live.

- ✔ Regardless of how difficult it is, do you have a sense of 'Yes, this is where I'm meant to be, doing exactly what I'm supposed to be doing with my life at this time'? While they may have had to deal with a lot of financial insecurity at the start, and risk losing friends and even family, our storytellers remained hopeful about the future – and that made a difference. They believed that it really would work out just right. For what they were now doing with their lives felt so right. Many speak of a feeling of having come home to themselves; that the life they were now living just felt right, difficult as it was at the start of the journey.

- ✔ Are you able to focus all your energy, thought and capital upon the new life you are living? The storytellers knew they were on the right tack because no matter how challenging it was at times, they had a sense of having done the right thing in pursuing the life they were now living. They enjoyed being the person they were becoming and this was something they wanted to hold on to. The sacrifices they had made meant that their new life was not something they were prepared to give up.

- ✔ Do you now have a sense that it is possible that the life you are now living could lead to amazing possibilities? For our storytellers, it was as if their new work was no longer just a job: it was more than that. They were no longer just going through the motions. There was now a feeling of being upbeat about life, as if there was a rejuvenation going on. They had gained some control over what was going on in their lives. And that, yes, this is what living the life you were born to live means.

- ✔ While the journey could be difficult at times, they still wanted to maintain this sense of being true to themselves – and for that reason alone they knew they were living the life they were meant to be living. They were finally doing what they wanted in their life and work, feeling truer to themselves and better about themselves. They were happier and felt freer to give their all in pursuit of the life they now wanted to live. It felt as if anything and everything was now possible.

Again, if you can answer 'yes' to any or all of the above questions, you are on the right tack and steering your life in the right direction it needs to be going for you.

While our storytellers have many things in common, they all had to give up the old life they had been living if they were to see the living out of why they were born become a reality in their everyday lives. They will tell you that there are still times when they feel bruised, battered and bloodied. Yet they keep getting up and going out each day to live their life and do their work as best they can. For they believe and accept that it is up to them to make their best lives happen. Regardless of the challenges they've had to face, they understand the need to keep going, enjoying the up times and accepting the down times.

The storytellers understood and accepted the necessity of never giving up on the journey of first figuring out why they were born and then making it a reality in the living out of it in their everyday lives. They also accepted that this journey rarely happens in a straight line – as was the case for Kate T. Lawler. Kate was expected to do well in her school exams and go straight to college and study law. When she didn't do so well, she was 'encouraged' to do a secretarial course instead. This was in a strange way to give a direction to her life that otherwise it probably would not have found. As we know, sometimes what seems to go against you might just in fact go for you! When Kate finished her secretarial course in 1971, she got a job in the general office of the oldest tobacco manufacturer in Ireland. Recognising quickly that Kate was smart, a quick learner and very observant, the company appointed her as the personal assistant to the marketing director the following year, when she was only eighteen years old.

At the age of twenty-four, Kate took the decision to give up her job and go to college as a full-time student. While she wanted to study Marketing and PR, she was a little before her time as only men did those sorts of jobs back then! Instead, she did a degree in Economics and Politics, expecting to return to her old employer once she had completed her studies; and, after graduating, she was offered her old job back. Only, not wanting to be a PA all her life, Kate was to make another brave decision and decline the offer. Having finished university and being without a job, she initially joined a temping agency. This had her working in several organisations, at many jobs with very different people. After Kate had been working for six weeks at Allied Irish Investment Bank, having initially gone to work there for a week, the bank offered her a job… as a PA.

Speaking to HR, Kate explained that she did not want to be a PA and that she wanted an opportunity to use her degree. They offered her a job as a lending executive. She accepted and became the first woman in this role within the bank. As in those days only men came looking for business loans, they would have been expecting to deal with a man. This being the case, Kate quickly had to gain their trust and make them believe that she was the person who could get a loan for them. Coming from a family business background, she already knew the ins and outs of running a small business.

In 1980, she met some people from California through her involvement with a folk group that sang at a church where a family friend was a priest. This was to lead to her and her friend Finola taking a holiday in California the following year. While there, a job offer was to come Kate's way. On her return to Ireland, she gave the job offer a lot of thought. This made her realise that she really was not enjoying the life she was living. Nor did she like the person she was becoming. Her work was making her become very hard as a person and financially driven. Not at all the individual she wanted to be. It was, in fact, making her go against all that she had learnt about life and her values. Likewise, she did not see herself achieving her full potential if she were to stay doing the work she was doing. Therefore, she made the decision to take the plunge and hand in her notice.

Six months later, Kate began a new life in California. After a few false starts, and some interesting experiences, including meeting many people from different cultural backgrounds, she was to end up in the most senior position for a laywoman in the Roman Catholic Church in California, working for the Archdiocese of Los Angeles as their Executive Director for Justice and Peace. Then, during Christmas time in 1986, through a series of coincidences and synchronicities, she was to reconnect with Colum who was to become her future husband. They had first met when they were both working for the tobacco manufacturer back in Ireland. The only problem now was that he was still living in Ireland and she in the States. So, after much travelling back and forth, with many long discussions about the best place for them and their family (as two new stepsons were now also going to be part of her story), they got married in California in 1989 and then settled in Ireland the following year.

Having moved back to Ireland in September 1990 without a job, Kate drew on the experience gained from her time in the States by working for herself in the mornings so as to be free for the two boys in the afternoon. Her work involved leading personal development courses for people living in disadvantaged and marginalised communities. This work and wanting to see people live their lives to the best of their abilities had Kate take on further roles in consultancy and senior management. Ready for a new challenge in 2014, she became the Deputy Director in a detention centre that provided a secure environment for young people to reduce their likelihood of reoffending.

In 2017, with her work finished at the centre where others were continuing what she had started, it was time for Kate to move on once again. Today, she is self-employed and brings all of her experience, learning, disappointments and triumphs to the work she now does, helping people to prepare for job interviews, their next role and the career they want to pursue. She loves every single moment of it, as do all those who get to work with her. As to the future and living her dream, she tells me:

> Yes, I am living the dream. Moreover, if this is to continue for me then it will mean having to keep on learning; the learning and training never stops. If I am to be of full service to each of the people who put their trust in me, I must keep growing and learning every day, recognising that this will allow me to go on meeting the

amazing people who come to me for what I do. This will keep me attending seminars, talks and reading at least one book a week. It will keep my mind sharp and challenged on both a personal and professional level, allowing me to bring all my knowledge, learning and life experience to each of my coaching clients in Potential Achieved. So, yes, this is exactly where I am meant to be – and that for me is living the dream.

Like Kate, many of our storytellers believed they were giving themselves the best chance of achieving all they now wanted to do by surrounding themselves with the right people. They understood that no one succeeds or fails alone, and that they had to pay attention to the people around them. Yet even if the right people were not in their life, they still needed to move forward and cultivate a strong support network with some good mentor(s).

Keep surrounding yourself with the right people when you are seeking to live your best life. Like our storytellers, be mindful of the need to work at hanging out with people who will support, encourage and assist you in living the life for which you were born and doing the work you are meant to be doing. Very often these people, like you, will be seeking to live the life for which they were born too, like Kate's clients are – or they might even be living it. For when you do find people who understand and support you, this will strengthen your motivation and push you forward to take the necessary action for you to go live your truth. Likewise, reading and listening to the right material will help you to get on the right tack and forge ahead in pursuit of the life you want to be living.

7. Forging Ahead

How You Can Too

If this book sets out to do anything, it is to share with you the stories of how ordinary people get to live extraordinary lives by doing what it is they were born to do. It aims to show how they were first able to figure out why they were born and then decide how best they could go live it. Just as you can do too; that is, if like them you are prepared to put in the time, effort and energy. So, are you ready now to figure out why you were born – and then go live it?

Our storytellers' experiences are a testament to the fact that, even when they had figured out why they were born, it could be difficult to live their truth. For if it were not, things would have often happened quicker, easier and a lot smoother for them than they did. Likewise, they regard this to be an ongoing process and that it may well take them a lifetime to achieve. Having figured out why you were born, will you likewise be prepared to deal with the challenge of bridging the gap between the life you are living and the life you want to live? If your answer is 'yes', congratulations and good luck! Only be warned, if you are waiting for the perfect moment, situation or job to make your move, you may well be in for a long wait. For it is not as if bridging this gap begins in an orderly fashion or at an appointed hour with rational, coherent, decisive action. It does not leave a platform like a train at a certain time and on schedule.

Bridging the gap between the storytellers' old lives to the lives they are now living was not at all straightforward, even though the storytellers' desire to be their best selves is all about going forward. There is still the on-going need for them to live with stumbling and falling backwards and with having to pick themselves up, dust themselves down and start again, repeatedly having to work at pushing their lives in the direction they truly want them to be going. Knowing all this, like the storytellers, do you now have the courage to:

- Figure out why you were born;
- Then look to see how best you can make a living from the life you were born to live;
- Take the necessary action to bridge the gap from the life you are living to the life you were born to live?

Can you do all this while knowing that when you go to take the first step, you will need to be on your guard as it can be a time of genuine doubt and fear? And can you accept that, regardless of any fears you have, once you do decide to make the change, it will be possible for you to live the life you were born to live – no matter how challenging it may get?

The fear never fully goes away, yet the waves of fear will eventually pass without engulfing you if you are prepared to hang in there and keep going when the going gets tough. By directing your attention, using your willpower and making the right decisions to deal with the challenges, you too will overcome them. Keep believing that you have what it takes to bring your life to where you now want it to be; that you have what it takes to deal with any disruptions that pursuing your new life could cause for you or those that matter most in your life; that you can deal with the challenges of making a living from what you intend to do, particularly at the start of your journey. Know that if it all goes wrong, you can deal with this and come back stronger and better able to handle whatever else life throws at you.

Well then, are you now at that point in your life where:

- ✔ You are ready to change the way that you are living?
- ✔ The life you are living is not enough for you anymore?
- ✔ Living as you are feels like lying to yourself?
- ✔ Living the way you are means not being true to yourself?

For the storytellers, the answers to these questions was a resounding 'yes', which then had them figure out why they were born and then go live it, regardless of what the future might hold. Yet even then, the thought was still there that it might just be easier to stick with the life they already knew, rather than pursue a new life with no guarantee of how it would all work out.

Having faced these sorts of doubts and challenges, many of our storytellers will tell you that, yes, at the start this new life of theirs sometimes seemed too hard to pursue, or had them thinking that the risk might not be worth it and they ought to go back to the life they already knew. So as not to give in to those moments, you too might have to learn early on to adhere to the course you have set yourself – just as they did. An important maxim to know is that the secret of successfully living out why you were born is not to panic; and particularly so in the early stages, when things might not go your way.

One brilliant way in which our storytellers dealt with these moments was the same as the way they dealt with fear and doubts: by surrounding themselves with good, positive, success-minded people. Like them, continually work at building your own tribe of people who will positively support and encourage you in the living out of the life that you now want to live.

With this in mind, here is one more question for you as we near the end of the book:

✔ Can you name the ten people with whom you spend most of your time? Beside each name, put a plus sign if they give you energy; a minus sign if they take your energy; and leave the space blank if their effect on you is neutral in that they neither give nor take energy. The people with the minus sign next to their names are the energy takers – and you need to remove them from your life. That is how tough it can be; or your relationship needs radically altering to make sure they have the minimum amount of impact on your wellbeing. In addition, commit to spending more time with those who give you energy.

While it is important to surround yourself with the right people, the truth is you will now have to forge your own path to bring your life to where you want it to be, regardless of who is in your life either now or in the future.

I hope the stories in these pages can act as a guide and support to you as you come to know and show your true colours and live the life you want to be living. For you, just as for our storytellers, there is no simple path to take. It has to be a path that you make as you forge ahead (once a naval term for progressing slowly, today the phrase is used to mean 'continuing' or 'to press on', but not always slowly). Like our storytellers, you will need to call upon your own courage, experience, and wisdom as you continue to pursue the path you need to follow to achieve the life you were born to live. There may well be a need to be gentle with yourself, especially at the start, as you learn to row the boat given to you to the best of your ability, in pursuit of the life you want to be living. Accept that as you forge ahead, life is short – and, as we know, tide and time wait for no one. With this in mind, what is the first action you can take to give yourself the best chance of living the life you were born to live?

All that is left for me to do is to wish you the very best for the future as you set out on your journey towards the life you were born to live. For in a world of heroes and legends (some more deserving than others), you will get to join the people telling their stories here – ordinary people living extraordinary lives, such as Olive 'Bibi' Baskin. Born in Donegal, Bibi got her nickname one summer while working in Germany as a student. Being fluent in Irish and having a love of the Irish language, she became a teacher when she left college. Then, in the mid 1980s, she became the editor of the Irish language newspaper Anois, which gave her a foothold in Dublin's media world. She went on to work for the national Irish broadcaster RTÉ, where she presented radio and television programmes, including her own chat show. She became a household name and went on to present The Saturday Show, giving her the distinction of being the first woman to host her own television chat show in Ireland. At that time she was being described in the media as 'The Special One'; yet eight years later, she was ready for a change. For she knew in her heart she could not stay in the same job or place for the rest of her life. She tells me:

> I'm forty-two and driving into the TV station as I had done five days a week, probably, you know, for the previous eight years, and I swung the car into the usual parking place and I found myself thinking, 'Wait a minute. Do I want to drive the car into the same place for another twenty years?' And I just said, 'No', and that was a light bulb moment for me. There was just no way could I nor would I want to go on doing the same thing day in after day out.

She continues:

> I knew then that I was going to go off and do something else. There was nothing wrong with the job. I had a great employer, it worked very well for me and I was very grateful for it. Only, like I said, I just couldn't do the same thing day in day out; I just couldn't countenance it – assuming, that is, my employer would have been happy to have me there for the next twenty or twenty-five years. This may make me sound very ungrateful, and I

wasn't; it was just that I can't stand boredom and when boredom starts to creep in I recognise it. And I'd say, 'Right, mate, you have to start making changes!'

So, with the excitement of new possibilities in the mid 1990s, I decided it was London for me, as I figured it was a very exciting and multicultural city with lots of opportunities and different scenarios and, hopefully, somewhere I could get a job in broadcasting.

Now, there are two ways you can do that: you can play it safe, and don't give up the first job or sell the house and car until you get the next job. Only my theory was one, Michael, of: if you wait until you check all those boxes, you're probably never do it. So I did it the unsafe way.

Furthermore, when a decision like this is made, you must show commitment to it. To show the evidence that you are going for it. And for me that was leaving the job I had without having a new one lined up, as well as selling my home and car. Furthermore, the house and car were about the only two things that I had loans on. As for so many of us, one of them shows the foundations of our existence in its own way, and we have the other because we need to get around. Only I was done. When I left, I left – and I was very happy with that. It didn't cause me any consternation because I was looking forward to what's next.

Therefore, I went off, having sold the house and the car, and initially moved to London, renting a room in the house of an elderly lady who was a friend of one of my sisters. With no work for about a year while trying to meet with people in the broadcasting world. I didn't really need to do fancy London life anyway because I didn't have an income.

Then the broadcasting work started to flow in and she ended up working for the BBC, Channel 5 and doing an afternoon show on ITV. She says:

> The only thing is London didn't feel like much of a change, as all I had really done was change geography. I was still doing broadcasting, living in an English-speaking country, and had been to London countless times before. It just didn't feel enough at all, as there was a big wide world out there and I wanted a little nibble of it. So, other than telling my best friend – and not anyone else, which I believe is great advice – I decided to leave London and once again sold my house and car, thinking that I would go on a brief holiday to clear the head, because I had no idea what I was going to do next.

> Only having the belief that if you have no fear about what you're going to do next, there's a good chance it will work for you. And I think it's very important that you bring that to bear on your next step, and that's why I can confidently say to you, Michael, I walked away looking forward to the next thing. Even if I did not know what it was going to be…

> So, I'm staying with friends in London, and I booked a three-week holiday to Kerala, in India, because for the previous twenty years, I had been an unofficial student of

Ayurveda, the wonderful Indian system of health and medicine that started in Kerala 5,000 years ago.

At forty-eight years of age, she made the 8,000km trip to Kerala. She was only intending to visit for three weeks but she ended up staying for fifteen years. She explains:

> A colleague of mine in London had been going there for about eight years, and knew a little seaside area. When he heard I was going and that this was going to be my first trip, he said I should come when he was there. So, I hooked up with him for two days. And he knew everybody in the locality and introduced me to the Ayurvedic doctor, the dentist, the shopkeeper and so many other people.
>
> It was great, I really liked it there, and the people were so very gentle. And I thought to myself, 'Sure, what am I going back to, really?' So, I rented a house, thinking I would stay for six months and write a book. Only, after six months I really did like it and decided to stay. Only, being Irish and a nation of house owners, you know, we don't feel secure unless we own our house. Even though it is the bank that really owns them! This had me envisage myself having my own house at that time with the stability that this would bring, along with writing the book (which didn't happen – the book that is, as I bought a house in 2001). Only the house needed refurbishment. It really was down at heel, but it was a landmark building in that area by the sea. And so, I spent a lot of time being a self-styled interior designer as I turned it into an Ayurvedic Wellness Centre, with the

intention of maybe having some guests come and stay at weekends that might be English and keep me company. Only, legally if you are changing your home into a business, you need to have it inspected. To make a long story short, the big tourist officials from Delhi inspected it and they said, 'You are now the proud owner of a heritage hotel of India.'

She's too modest to say that in fact it was to go on and be named one of the Best Sleeps in India in the Sunday Times, which it did. She continues:

There was something else at work that was far more important than confidence for me at that time, and that was, I did not know if this project would work or not. I had no experience in the hospitality industry and this was being done in a faraway developing country, working with people whose first language was not English. And the trick was that I didn't care if I failed or succeeded. I truly didn't care.

When people fail, they can too often feel ashamed and that people will look down on them. Yet, most people are so caught up in their own lives they really think little about what is or is not going on for you or me. So, really, what they think does not matter. The couple of really good friends we all have in life will always be there, even if you do fail.

So, what is there to worry about if you fail? Yes, you'll be out of pocket and yes, you must lick your wounds. Only go into that job, saying to yourself, 'I don't care if I fail.' So, I was quite carefree and not taking it at all too seriously. I really think that was the one singular piece of psychological armour that saw me through.

Then, after fifteen years, there no longer remained any intrigue in running a hotel. It was all becoming too familiar. This, combined with the fact that I was getting older, had me wanting to come back home to Ireland. I was in my early sixties and that was reason enough to want life to be easier as well.

While there was no light bulb moment in Bibi's decision to come back home to Ireland, it did mean she had to bide her time. For, as she told me:

When you get it into your head that you want to make a big change, you might just have to learn to be patient, because it can take a little while or even longer for the circumstances to allow you to follow through on your decision and see the change you want to become a reality. In my case, house prices were rising once again at a really fast rate in Ireland. And on my modest Indian salary, I couldn't have afforded the house that I kind of wanted.

About two years after Bibi's decision to come back to Ireland, it was possible for her to do so, and she was able to buy a house she liked in West Cork, where she is now enjoying life. As she will tell you, it is a place that has welcomed her with open arms. As for what is next for her, she tells me:

One of my greatest pleasures is studying, so as an eternal student I will continue to go on learning every day. To go on making little videos around wellness and sharing them on social media. To keep writing, having already published two books, and to also take time to do nothing – to be very busy being non-busy and just take time to still the mind. Likewise, being passionate about food and cooking, who knows what might come from this in the future?

Bibi really is a force of nature who is grateful for the things that have happened to her and that she has made happen. Like her and the other storytellers in this book, you too can figure out why you were born and then go and live it, if you are prepared to:

- Accept that there will be many ups and downs along the way and, in all probability, things will not happen in a straight line;
- Tell very few people initially of your decision and plans to go live the life you were born to live;
- Be very grateful and appreciate your good fortune if you have a partner who will support you in the living out of the life you were born to live and the work you want to be doing;
- Accept and take the necessary risks involved in pursuing the life you want to be living;
- Stop sitting around and just go for it once you have made the decision to live the life you were born to live;
- Understand and accept that your life will be more of a marathon than a sprint in pursuit of all that you now want to achieve;

- Surround yourself with the right people and read the right books that will enable you in living the life and doing the work that you were born to do.

So then, like those telling their stories here, are you now ready to embrace all of the above considerations and go and live the life you were born to live? If your answer to this is 'yes', well then, all that is left for me to do is to wish you the very best as you begin to live the life you were born to live and show your true colours!

Epilogue

COVID-19 brought a time of worry and uncertainty for all of us. You may well be wondering how the storytellers are doing since COVID-19 hit, particularly those with their own businesses. If you would like to know how they are doing now on their journeys, please visit my website, www.michaeldalyireland.com, where you will get to meet and hear how all of them dealt with COVID-19.

There are moments in life that can be ripe for change, as was the case for so many of those sharing their stories in this book. A time of stoppage – be it from having to face illness, a great disappointment, the collapse of a business, being made redundant, death, or the failure of a relationship – can nevertheless offer fresh opportunities. And with COVID-19 often been referred to as a 'once-in-a-century event', might this be your own stoppage moment. A time that has you figure out why you were born and then go live your truth. And have you showing your own true colours at last too.

Michael E. Daly

July 2022

Acknowledgements

I would like to thank all who have shared their stories with me, in particular those whose stories made this book possible. It was a challenge to put their stories into such a few words, which is what I have had to do here – and any mistakes are truly mine alone. I am so grateful to every one of you. You have allowed this book become the reality it is and, for doing so, thank you Danny Range, Steven Farrell, Daniela Enzinger, Tom Dalton, Krissy and Kevin Gibson, Amandine Passot Devine, Adrian Haines, Martin Deporres Wright, Medbh Boyle, Sharon Rossignuolo, Barry Kirwan, Ann Keenaghan, K. T. Lawlor and Bibi Baskin.

Big thanks to Sue Lascelles, who helped to turn this into the book you are reading.

I am so very grateful to Peter Freeth of Genius Media, for his ongoing faith in me and for letting this book become the reality it is.

www.ingramcontent.com/pod-product-compliance
Lightning Source LLC
Chambersburg PA
CBHW031451040426
42444CB00007B/1054